Paris in Turmoil

Paris in Turmoil

A City between Past and Future

Éric Hazan

Translated by David Fernbach

VERSO
London • New York

This book is supported by the Institut français
(Royaume-Uni) as part of the Burgess programme.

INSTITUT
FRANÇAIS
ROYAUME-UNI

First published in English by Verso 2022
Translation © David Fernbach 2022
First published as *Le tumulte de Paris*, Editions La Fabrique, 2021

Verso
UK: 6 Meard Street, London W1F 0EG
US: 388 Atlantic Avenue, Brooklyn, NY 11217
versobooks.com

Verso is the imprint of New Left Books

ISBN-13: 978-1-83976-466-0
ISBN-13: 978-1-83976-471-4 (US EBK)
ISBN-13: 978-1-83976-470-7 (UK EBK)

British Library Cataloguing in Publication Data
A catalogue record for this book is available from the British Library

Library of Congress Cataloging-in-Publication Data
A catalog record for this book is available from the Library of Congress

Typeset in Sabon by MJ & N Gavan, Truro, Cornwall
Printed and bound by CPI Group (UK) Ltd, Croydon, CR0 4YY

Contents

Preface

This book was undertaken to defend Paris, which is so bad-mouthed today – a museum city, sluggish, gentrified, etc. The worst thing is that these remarks are made not just by the usual enemies of Paris, those who keep their distance, afraid of its periodic explosions. But that people whom Paris has sheltered, educated and cultivated, people who are basically indebted to it for what they have become, also participate in this denigration of their mother city. Perhaps there is a certain justification in this way of debunking Paris, of ruining the myth. Museum city? It is true that someone standing at the centre of the Pont-Neuf and turning full circle could get the impression of being in the gigantic hall of an imaginary museum. But there is nothing new about this; Rastignac or Baudelaire would have had more or less the same view – at least apart from the Samaritaine department store. Gentrification? For a long time now, Paris has been divided in two by a line running roughly through Rue du Faubourg-Poissonnière and Rue Poissonnière, with the '*beaux quartiers*' to the west and the 'popular' neighbourhoods to the east. During the great proletarian uprising of June 1848, this was the farthest line reached by the workers' barricades.

What is true is that, since the disastrous Pompidou years, working-class Paris has been steadily nibbled away, either by destruction (the Vel d'Hiv where the great Six Jours fair with Édith Piaf and Marcel Cerdan was held; the Place des Fêtes, where restaurant regulars still had their personal napkin rings in 1960; Rue Watt and its surroundings, dear to the Situationists), or, more insidiously, by a kind of internal colonization. Take for example a small outlying district populated by Arabs,

Blacks and poor whites twenty years ago, the Olive neighbourhood north of La Chapelle (I could have taken other examples,
the banks of the Canal Saint-Martin thirty years ago or Place
de la Réunion today). The area is noted as pleasant, people
frequent it and explore it, and as the rents are low some settle
there. Others follow, first friends and then anyone else. Rents
go up, buildings are renovated, bars open, then an organic
food shop, a vegan restaurant ... The inhabitants are driven
out by the rising rents and settle further away, in Saint-Denis
if they are lucky, or else in Garges-lès-Gonesse, Goussainville
or God knows where. So working-class neighbourhoods are
colonized by people who have no bad intentions – on the contrary, they are delighted to live in a 'colourful' neighbourhood
and regret seeing it go all white.

If capitalism continues to prosper, the process will end up
emptying Paris of all its poor and extend to the first ring of the
banlieues where they have migrated. But, if we are at the end
of a cycle that began with Thermidor – and there are many
signs leading us to hope for this – then everything will become
possible again, including the return of the excluded, the over-
crowded, the despised. In the meantime, we must keep a grip
on the city, know its history and its vagaries, so that when the
time comes it can regain its colours and its glory. That is the
purpose of this book.

It has a model: the *Tableau de Paris* by Louis-Sébastien
Mercier, whose last volumes were published in 1788. Without
seeking to match this admirable work, I have borrowed from it
the idea of short, discontinuous texts on subjects that vary from
one page to another. I reworked these a little and left them in
the order in which they were written. I have not spoken about
the upheavals in Parisian life brought about by the current pan-
demic. Others have done so – particularly at La Fabrique – and
I did not feel it necessary to add my grain of salt.

Neighbourhoods

On paper, Paris is divided into eighty *quartiers*, four per arrondissement, but this division is purely administrative, lacking any palpable reality. No one will tell you that they live in Gros-Caillou or Sainte-Marguerite. What they consider 'their neighbourhood' is an emotional territory whose boundaries may be historically and geographically clear without everyone giving it the same name. Thus, some people will say they live in the Marais, while their near neighbours will say they live on Rue Saint-Antoine or 'not far from Bastille'.

Some neighbourhoods have changed so much that they no longer justify their traditional names. The Latin Quarter, where tourists outnumber students, centred on a Sorbonne where you have to show your identity card to get in, and deprived of almost all its large bookshops, no longer has much Latin about it. In the Jewish quarter of Rue des Rosiers, there are only two or three shops where you can still find *gefilte fish* or *pastrami*, as the old Ashkenazi population have died and their children gone to live elsewhere. The Goldenberg charcuterie, once a neighbourhood flagship, has given way to a Japanese fashion shop. Some neighbourhoods have even disappeared completely: in the former Armenian neighbourhood, around Rue Lamartine and Rue de Trévise, all that remains are a few shop signs with an Armenian sound.

Many once large communities never had their own neighbourhoods. The White Russians, very numerous in Paris from the 1920s to the 1950s, also had a newspaper whose theatre critic was the owner of a Russian restaurant on Rue Bréa, 'Chez Dominique'. White Russians were often taxi drivers – beret pulled down to the ears, grey overcoat, dead Gitane, and a very particular way of mistreating their old black and red G7 taxi. This community evaporated without having had a definite location in the city, and is all but forgotten – a pity.

But other neighbourhoods are emerging. New Jewish districts have developed, one at the bottom of Rue Manin near Porte Chaumont, the other, posher, in the seventeenth arrondissement around Avenue de Wagram, Rue Rennequin and Rue Jouffroy-d'Abbans. Older already is the 'Indian' district, in fact Sri Lankan and mainly Tamil, whose shops for saris and Tamil-language films are on Rue du Faubourg-Saint-Denis between the Gare du Nord and Place de la Chapelle. The Kurds (so-called Turks) have for years had their neighbourhood in the tenth arrondissement, on Rue d'Enghien, Rue de l'Echiquier and at the bottom of Rue Saint-Denis. Even older (though less old than the large complex in the thirteenth arrondissement) is the Chinese quarter of Bas Belleville, which has grown since the 1970s to the point that, in some streets, such as Rue Civiale or Rue Rampal, the restaurants and shops are all Chinese, with many Chinese sex workers on Boulevard de la Villette. These 'Chinese' almost all come from Wenzhou, a large province south of Shanghai, whose inhabitants are reputedly known for their commercial skills.

'Paris is no longer what it used to be' – yes, and fortunately it changes and constantly evolves like a living organism, some parts atrophying while others proliferate.

Tabacs and Droguistes

The poor smoke more than the rich. Sociological studies show this, but we scarcely need them: just compare the density of tobacconists between fashionable Paris and working-class neighbourhoods. Between the Palais-Bourbon and the Institut du Monde Arabe there are only three tobacconists on the elegant Boulevard Saint-Germain, including the Cave des Cigares at the Odéon crossroads, which is not really a *bureau de tabac*. Three is the number of tobacconists on Rue de Belleville, between Métro station Belleville and the next one, Pyrénées, a five-minute walk away. Like obesity, smoking is a marker of class. In fact, it is rare for *bureaux de tabac*, often also hosting the PMU, Loto and Française des Jeux,* to be chic establishments – like the Civette, opposite the Comédie Française, where state councillors probably go to buy their Havana cigars.

The names of Parisian tobacconists sometimes refer to their location – Tabac du Roule, de la Muette, des Gobelins – but often take the name of brands of cigar or cigarette that have long since disappeared, dating back to the time when dark tobacco emerged by the ton from the SEITA factories and was smoked in all the cafés. *Week-end, Balto, Reinitas, Celtic, Boyard*: so many memories from the years of the Renault Dauphine, Jean-Luc Godard's *Petit Soldat* and Romain Gary's Prix Goncourt for *Les Racines du ciel*. As for the name 'Le

---

* Pari Mutuel Urbain is a syndicate of companies offering off-course betting on horse races; Loto is the Lotérie Nationale, the most popular offering of Française des Jeux, a company with majority state ownership. – Translator.

Jean-Bart', this refers to the legend of the famous corsair threatening his English jailers to set fire to a powder keg with the lit cigar he was holding in his hand.

In those years, Parisian tobacconists were often run by natives of Auvergne, or more precisely of the Rouergue – not very friendly, on the whole, with big wolfhounds and surly wives. Almost nothing remains of this population, the rare 'Au Bougnat'* signs being rather souvenirs of wood and coal merchants, who have also almost disappeared. There is indeed a *tabac* called Le Rouergue on Rue du Faubourg-du-Temple, but the owner is Chinese and does not know why his establishment bears this name. All smokers and lottery-ticket scratchers are aware how, for several years now, Paris *tabacs* have been massively taken over by Chinese. They are often young, and far more pleasant and efficient than the old ones from Villeneuve-sur-Lot. When asked about the reasons for this Asian domination of such a Parisian business, their answers are unclear: a system of tontines to raise the necessary money (a well-placed *tabac* can cost up to a million euros) or the ability to work harder than others.

More curious is that Paris *droguistes*, those hardware stores where you can find mothballs, plungers, mousetraps and so many other useful objects, often have an Indian from Madagascar as their owner. In a beautiful establishment on Rue Choiseul, near the Opéra Comique, one of these explained this penchant to me: 'In India, we belong to a caste whose speciality is precisely these shops where everything is sold. Many of us settled in Madagascar in the French time, and our families had shops like this one. And when we had to leave, the choice naturally fell on France. Today, when a *droguiste* comes up for sale, we try to get one of our people to take it.' Provided they continue, and manage to resist the chains of Leclerc, Auchan and the like, we shall still have these shops where, as with certain old garages or second-hand wind

---

* '*Bougnat*' is a traditional term for migrants to Paris from the Massif Central. – Trans.

instrument dealers, an ordered accumulation defies standardization and rivals in its fantasy the contemporary art forms known as installations.

Kiosks and Carts

The newsagent by the Belleville Métro station explains to me how, at around four in the morning, his suppliers drop their packets into a box at the back of his kiosk which they have a key to. So he never sees them – except the one from *Le Monde*, who comes by at about half past twelve.

Until the 1960s, the press district was concentrated between Rue Réaumur, Rue Montmartre and Boulevard Poissonnière: *L'Aurore* on Rue Montmartre, *L'Humanité* on Boulevard Poissonnière, *Le Parisien libéré* and *France-Soir* on Rue Réaumur, *Le Monde* almost in exile at the end of the small Rue des Italiens. As soon as the newspapers came off the presses, swarms of cyclists set off to distribute them to the kiosks on bikes with smaller front wheels to accommodate an enormous metal rack. (In the days when meat was delivered to homes, the butcher's boys had similar bicycles, but they were red.) The cyclists were not the only ones to distribute newspapers, there were also street sellers who sold them retail in the busiest places – Métro stations, cinema queues, railway stations, department stores, the Champs-Elysées (Jean Seberg selling the *Herald Tribune* in Godard's *À bout de souffle*). A little later, around 1960, the bicycles were replaced by motorbikes, BMWs with sidecars in which the bundles of newspapers were stacked.

And then everything changed, when the printing works moved out of the city centre. Newspapers ceased to be places where the editorial, typesetting, proofreading and printing departments were located on different floors of the same building. From now on, delivery could only be made in anonymous and not very picturesque vans from increasingly distant suburbs.

Bicycles with a small front wheel are not the only vehicles to have sunk to the bottom of memories. I remember that, after the war, the Gervais dairy used to deliver milk to the shops on large wooden floats fitted with pneumatic tyres and pulled by two horses. Large milk cans would jostle against each other, and litre containers attached to a long metal rod hung from the rim of these cans. It was said that Monsieur Gervais was very fond of horses.

As long as Les Halles remained in Paris, fruit and vegetable carts were to be found all over the city. So-called '*marchands de quatre saisons*' would stock up at the large central market, pushing their loads to their regular point of sale, a street market or elsewhere. These wooden carts, always painted green, had two large iron-rimmed wheels at the front and a stand at the back to stabilize the cart when stationary. Two long wooden handles were used to pull it or push. This is an image of the Parisian landscape that has long disappeared, known only from the photographs of Doisneau and a few others.

And the marvellous square Renault two-coloured taxis – red up to the door handles, black above – with a comfort bordering on luxury. Separated from the driver by a sliding window (as in London), you would sit on a bench covered with a thick cloth, almost a carpet, that was magnificent in my memory. The meter was outside, and the driver had to roll down his window to reach it. With each new customer, he would re-set it with a key placed just below the numbers, which scrolled by during the journey, franc after franc. I can still hear the very peculiar sound of the key winding the spring of the meter. A small panel the size of a business card was placed obliquely on the meter at the start of the journey, the only indication that the taxi was no longer free.

You also took the bus. Entrance and exit were through the same door at the back, on a platform open to the elements. The ticket collector punched the tickets with a metal device held against his stomach by a strap. Here, again, I can hear the sound of this machine. The ticket collector would give the driver the signal to leave by pulling on a chain with a wooden handle attached to a bell. When the bus was full, police and firefighters could still ride 'extra', standing at the edge of the platform holding on to the metal posts. Raymond Queneau's *Exercices de style* are set on a bus platform from the earliest era – an S-line bus before letters were replaced by numbers.

Beggars

To embark on a typology of dire poverty in Paris would be offensive to those who sleep on flattened cardboard boxes on the ground and find food in the dustbins. It is ourselves, the non-beggars, who should be written about.

One particular category is people who never give anything, ever, not even a cigarette. They are not necessarily heartless – they have arguments: pity is a sad passion and charity abjection; it is not by distributing a few euros at random that you fight against poverty; that's just a cheap way of giving yourself a good conscience. All that is fair enough, and those who still respond to a request by digging into their pockets know it very well. But, even beyond theoretical reticence, the question remains: to whom should we give?

It's not possible to give to everyone who puts out their hand. A gift is not just about putting a coin in that hand – or into a cup, a bowl, a cap. To give the gesture a minimum of meaning, it must be accompanied by a few words, a smile, a pat on the shoulder – in short, little signs showing a common belonging to the group of human beings. But gestures like this are not designed for repetition at every crossroads. Choices have to be made. Each to his own, so I'll talk about mine.

I have had several regular 'clients'. In the queue for the line 11 bus in Belleville, a man in his fifties, African, who plays the mandolin, or rather, plays notes very quietly without embarking on a melody, bent over the instrument, without a glance at the 'audience' – the rare times I've met him unbent, I could see that he is very tall and limps. A woman beggar has her head-quarters on a bench, near the great 1930 post office on Rue des Archives – the first time I saw this old lady, I was struck by the colour of her eyes, the kind that project blue all around them. When I am in the neighbourhood, I make a diversion to see if she is at her post and chat for a while.

These are exceptions, and most of those I give to are anonymous to me – which does not mean they are chosen at random. I can't resist those who approach me calmly and ask if I can help them: neither the young women veiled in black, strictly mute and motionless in a pose that is probably traditional, crouching, arm outstretched, elbows resting on the knees, hand open in the shape of a cup – beautiful like Egyptian statues; nor the Roma accordionists in the Métro who express their virtuosity in airs from back home instead of the usual tunes vaguely inspired by Piaf or Aznavour. In short, I give to the most charming, the most gifted, or who best wield their misfortune. Obviously, this is not what should be done. It would be better to help a little those who have least of all, the one whose melody pursues you mercilessly along the corridors, the one who starts the fatal speech in the Métro carriage, 'Excuse me for bothering you, my name is Robert, I am homeless.' Yes, but emotion often prevails over reason.

Portes

In order to unite the twenty arrondissements of Paris with the surrounding communes, one step is essential: remove the *portes* that separate them. A gate always means an inside and an outside, there is no getting away from it. And the encircling Périphérique, with its slip roads everywhere, reinforces the 'gate effect'. It would not be the first time that gates around Paris have been removed in order to enlarge the city. In the 1860s, when the communes that today make up the bulk of the double-digit arrondissements – from Ivry to Vaugirard on the Left Bank, Auteuil to Bercy on the Right – were annexed to Paris, the gates (usually called *barrières*) were removed. In the most important locations, the *barrière* was transformed into a large square included in the fabric of the new Paris: Place d'Italie, Place Denfert-Rochereau, Place de Stalingrad, Place des Ternes – among others – developed around the former *barrières* of Italie, Enfer, La Villette and Les Ternes.

Many of today's *portes* are mere intersections, such as Porte de Châtillon, Porte de Sèvres, Porte des Poissonniers or Porte Montmartre. The removal of the Périphérique and the improvement of its trajectory would transform them into ordinary urban crossroads, but to mark this change in status, their names would have to be changed – and there is no shortage of forgotten names, from Robespierre and Marx (who are not exactly forgotten) to Rimbaud, Freud, Mahler or Picasso. Often, the suburban communes, especially the formerly 'red' ones, have made up for these absences – thanks are in order.

For the larger *portes*, there is a huge difference between the west, where they are almost already squares – I have in mind Porte Saint-Cloud, Porte d'Auteuil and even Porte

Dauphine – and the northern and eastern *portes*, a nightmare for pedestrians and cyclists, sinks of ugliness, noise and pollution. All share the same material equipment: the Périphérique and its slip roads, one or more petrol stations as well as car washes, several Métro exits, countless traffic signs, two tram stations, several bus line terminals, some with three-digit numbers that leave for the banlieues and others with two-digit numbers that are internal Paris lines. All this in an unstructured space where the traffic between the Périphérique and the Boulevards des Maréchaux merges as best it can with the radial traffic, that of unfortunate people trying to get out of or into Paris. Transforming such spaces into squares is obviously difficult and sometimes even impossible: the Porte de la Chapelle, for example, with the tangle at ground level and above of the Périphérique, its slip roads, the tramway and the railway bridge linking the networks from the Gare de l'Est and the Gare du Nord.

Let us take a less unfavourable case, that of the Porte d'Orléans. Here, the square is almost sketched out by the two magnificent HBMs* at the corners with Boulevard Jourdan on the left and Boulevard Brune on the right: these two massive structures are placed at an angle, and if we were to continue them mentally, we would have a circle. But beyond the HBMs, the axial route opens out and gives way to a dingy public garden at the end of which stands the bronze statue of Marshal Leclerc. This has its back to the Périphérique, copied on the Montrouge side by Boulevard Romain-Rolland. It would not be so difficult to complete the square that has been sketched out by extending the belt of HBMs with a curve of buildings leaving between them a road the same width as Avenue du Maréchal-Leclerc on the Paris side. Behind the square, a row of low-rise buildings on the site of the Périphérique could make up for the ugliness of the metal and glass buildings on Boulevard Romain-Rolland.

---

* *Habitation à bon marché*, a prewar form of social housing later replaced by *habitations à loyer modéré* (HLM). – Translator.

Belleville

When we say Belleville, what exactly do we mean? I know some people who live on Rue Saint-Maur or Rue Jean-Pierre-Timbaud and are convinced that they live in Belleville, as if this name were linked to an atmosphere rather than a geographical boundary. In reality, the old commune of Belleville, annexed to Paris in 1860, extended on the Paris side as far as the Wall of the Farmers-General, or, in today's terms, as far as Boulevard de Belleville and Boulevard de Ménilmontant. At the other end, it ran as far as what became Boulevard Mortier and the Porte des Lilas. A large territory, therefore, which was not homogeneous, encompassing under the same name several different neighbourhoods linked by a great east-west axis, the long Rue de Belleville – 'Rue de Paris' in the former commune (as today in Montreuil, so well described by Jean-Christophe Bailly, shop after shop, in a book entitled simply *La rue de Paris*). At the very top is the neighbourhood of the Télégraphe Métro station – Chappe's optical telegraph, logically located at the highest point in Paris – and the Belleville cemetery, flanked by the two large water towers so often photographed. On the way down, you reach Place des Fêtes. Around 1960, this was still a neat little round square, a village square. The wasteland that today bears the name Place des Fêtes is the result of one of the worst urban planning attacks fomented under – and by – the enemy of Paris, Georges Pompidou. 'I believe,' wrote Guy Debord in *Panegyric*, 'this city was ravaged a little before all the others because its ever-renewed revolutions had so worried and shocked the world'.* After this disaster,

---

* Guy Debord, *Panegyric, Volumes 1 and 2* (London: Verso, 2004), p. 38.

continuing down Rue de Belleville, you enter a neighbourhood named Jourdain, after the Métro station and a small
street where one of the best bookshops in Paris, L'Atelier, is
located. This neighbourhood, dominated by a rather ugly neo-
gothic church (the work of Lassus, who also has his street
here) is unusual in Belleville: an island with a white population whereas everywhere else Blacks, Arabs and Chinese are
in the majority. At the Pâtisserie de l'Église, you would think
you were in Bourges or Montluçon – the cakes are very good,
as are the products offered by the neighbouring shops, pricier
than elsewhere in Belleville.

Further down again, after crossing Rue des Pyrénées, you
gradually enter the Chinatown which established itself here
in the 1970s and has been growing ever since. It gradually
thickens after Rue Jouye-Rouve (where the best and friend-
liest restaurant in Belleville and even beyond, Le Baratin, is
located) and Rue Rébeval (where the office of La Fabrique
is located). From Rue Julien-Lacroix, the main north-south
axis of Belleville, everything is Asian, if not always Chinese –
Thais, Vietnamese, Japanese and Koreans have merged with
the Chinese flood. Restaurants, food shops, mobile phone
dealers, manicurists, massages, costume jewellery, hairdress-
ers, florists – everything is Chinese except for two bakeries, a
branch of the Caisse d'Épargne and a pharmacy – where one
of the pharmacists is always Chinese.

At the very bottom of Rue de Belleville, you reach a large
crossroads punctuated by the five exits of the Belleville Métro
station. This crossroads deserves to be treated as a square,
but it curiously has no name, whereas many much smaller
sites close by bear the names of Jean Ferrat, Henri Krasucki
or Hannah Arendt – I would suggest calling it Place Frantz
Fanon. It is almost square-shaped, just cut short by the small
and very Chinese Rue Louis Bonnet. Rue du Faubourg-du-
Temple and Rue de Belleville meet here, across what was
for a long time the Belleville *barrière*; they merge into each
other gently, which is not always the case in such a layout:
Rue du Faubourg-Saint-Antoine is quite a way from Rue

Saint-Antoine, and Rue du Faubourg-Poissonnière from Rue Poissonnière.

The corner between Boulevard de Belleville and Rue du Faubourg-du-Temple (on the left looking towards Paris) is occupied by a large building probably dating from the 1920s. At street level, this is Chen Market, a huge food supermarket, and on the first floor, a restaurant displaying its name in big letters: Le Président. (Mao?) The corner opposite, between Boulevard de la Villette and the Faubourg, also has a large building but one difficult to date: reminiscent of a neoclassical edifice from the late eighteenth century, though the very high arcade at the entrance, rising to second-floor level, sows doubt. On the ground floor there was a Quick hamburger joint, now replaced by a Sephora.

The corner between Boulevard de la Villette and Rue de Belleville, to the north-east of the square, used to be marked by a café, Le Point du Jour, which can be seen in old photos where sometimes you can also see the steam funicular that 'descended cautiously from the church of Saint-Jean-Baptiste to Place de la République, and slowly and shakily creaked up again – for ten centimes it would take you through Rue du Faubourg-du-Temple and Rue de Belleville', Eugène Dabit wrote in *Les faubourgs de Paris*. This corner is now made ugly by the CFDT building, padlocked and surrounded by a metal fence that prevents access to a small garden. The edge of this fence is too narrow to sit comfortably, but, despite this, you often see old Chinese workers, tramps and drug addicts, with their backs to the fence and elbows on their knees.

The fourth corner, between Boulevard de Belleville and the Rue de Belleville, is occupied by a large café, wide open on both sides, called La Vielleuse. The building is no longer the one from which Jules Vallès fired on the Versaillais during the last days of the Commune, as he recounts in *L'Insurgé*; this was demolished and not too badly rebuilt in the 2000s. Above all, care has been taken to preserve the icon that gives its name to the place: a painting representing a hurdy-gurdy player, its glass broken by a piece of German shrapnel during the First

World War. The clientele varies according to the time of day and the day of the week, mostly Arab on market days (Tuesday and Friday), often Tunisian-Jewish (ageing, alas), Chinese at all times, including the ladies who trade their bodies on Boulevard de la Villette. The atmosphere in this café is noisy and harmonious: despite the diversity of population, I have never seen an argument here, I would even say never heard a cross word (I don't know all the languages spoken here, but there is always a special tone for insults that can easily be spotted).

Almost opposite La Vielleuse, at the end of the central strip with the market stalls, there is a merry-go-round with planes, horses and cars, where I spent a fortune when my daughter Cléo was very young. A little further on, the right side of Boulevard de Belleville (looking towards Père-Lachaise) is occupied by a large primary school, formerly the École Supérieure de Dessin, which no doubt explains the medallions on the façade representing Péguy, Jules Ferry, Jaurès, Debussy, Camille Claudel, Sadi Carnot, Émile Zola, Pasteur and Marie Curie, a whole secular and republican era. On the opposite pavement stands a large synagogue called Or-Hahaim, whose faithful are wrapped in coats and wear the large black hats their forefathers wore in Vilna. There is another much smaller and more discreet synagogue nearby, at the corner of Rue Julien-Lacroix and Rue de Pali-Kao. The men here wear a kepi, which evokes the time when the flag of the CGT union of coffin-makers had its motto written in Yiddish.

An Anecdote

This dates in part from the time when the corner of Boulevard de la Villette and Rue du Faubourg-du-Temple was occupied by a branch of Quick. A few months ago, an Arab singer was invited to perform in the garden opposite the Montreuil town hall, on the occasion of a 'national week of education against racism and anti-Semitism'. Rasheed's first song, *Louange,* was entirely in Arabic. According to Rasheed, from the very first words, the councillor in charge of organizing the event 'became visibly agitated, and started waving at me to stop singing.' (I wasn't there myself but I was told about it, and it was reported in the *Courrier de l'Atlas.*) 'She told me that I didn't have the right to sing this song, that we are in a community and that she has political responsibilities.'

Now, it so happens that I know this woman. About fifteen years ago, La Fabrique published a book on girls and the headscarf, a collection of testimonies gathered by three authors, including her, who at the time was still steeped in religion and wore a headscarf. After the book was published, she had a falling out with a bookshop in Montreuil whose manager, she said, if he did not actually hit her, at least treated her violently. As the affair was threatening to escalate, I went to find the guy, a Black Maoist, who told me that one day he had indeed pushed her towards the door: he was fed up with her incursions and repeated complaints (I have forgotten the reasons). Subsequently, the complainer and the book's coordinating editor formally requested me to condemn the violent bookseller. I remember a kind of tribunal in that famous Quick: I perceived in this woman a mixture of madness and spite, and so, after a while, I got up and went home. Afterwards, I was accused by many people of Islamophobia, which was quite amusing.

And now here is the same woman, bare-headed, a town councillor, refusing to let people sing in Arabic in a public place, presented as a bulwark of whiteness against the barbarians. About a famous ex-Stalinist columnist who moved in the 1990s from *L'Humanité* to the culture pages of *Figaro Magazine*, Vidal-Naquet said: 'You don't change jobs just because you change pavements.'

Bookshops

The irreplaceable André Schiffrin, author of, among others, *The Business of Books* (Verso, 2001), tells how, in order to pay for his studies, he worked in one or another of the 300 or so independent bookshops in New York around 1960. Today, you don't even need the fingers of one hand to count them, likewise in London for that matter. Berlin is a little better off, but in no way comparable to Paris, where the network of bookshops is the densest and best in the world. If several important ones have closed over the last twenty years – La Hune in Saint-Germain-des-Prés, the PUF bookshop on Place de la Sorbonne, Le Moniteur on Place de l'Odéon – beautiful and good bookshops have recently opened in unlikely corners, in the Sentier (La Petite Égypte) or the Goutte d'Or (La Régulière).

Since the beginning of the twenty-first century, population movements – sociological upheavals if you like – have changed the areas where Paris bookshops prosper, which had remained more or less the same since the youth of Paul Léautaud or André Breton. Montparnasse with its Jewish psychoanalysts and old Russian painters, Saint-Germain des Prés with its writers and publishers, were their strongholds. Now the old people are dead, the publishers have moved to the outskirts and rents have reached such levels that only the really rich can live in these neighbourhoods – classy foreigners, 'managers' with pointed shoes or directors of PR, not great book buyers on the whole. And, so, the book world's centre of gravity has shifted from the Left Bank to the north-eastern quarter of the city, between Rue du Faubourg-Montmartre and Rue du Faubourg-Saint-Antoine, with the hills of Belleville,

Ménilmontant and Charonne as its epicentre. Within a few hundred metres, there is a remarkable collection of bookshops that cultivate neither elitist snobbery nor pessimism about the future of books and reading.

It's easy to find a good bakery or bike shop, but a good bookshop? You might think that a good one means the greatest chance of finding the book you are looking for. This is partly true but not completely so, because it confuses a good bookshop with a *big* one – one that has a lot of space, a lot of money, a lot of titles, but is not necessarily *good*. You could even say that size has nothing to do with it. The quality of a bookshop can be seen right away from its window display. If this gives a feeling of coherence, if there is a clear logic in the choice: come on in, it's a good bookshop. The person who put together this window has created a network between authors and between titles, a mental network that is worth all social networks. When you enter, you will probably find other books on the tables that are also connected to one another. As Roland Alberto, a bookseller in Marseille, put it, 'The objective that every bookseller must aspire to is a shop in which each book is connected to the others by a thread made of encounters, readings, speculations, oppositions, errors, mistakes and footnotes' (*Le livre, que faire?*, La Fabrique, 2008). Contrary to what one might think, the profession of bookseller is one of the most personal there is, and if no point of view emerges from a walk around the tables, then you are in a shop selling books and not in a bookshop.

Left Bank

The Left Bank is a special case. I'm talking about the historic Left Bank, the Latin Quarter, Saint-Germain-des-Prés and Montparnasse, a district where the glory of Paris as capital of arts and letters had long been maintained. These neighbourhoods have now been unified and homogenized by the proliferation of clothes shops and restaurants, all middle range with a few luxury islands. Little or nothing happens there any more, whereas, in my youth, it was the centre of intellectual and artistic life. The good bookshops, the best jazz clubs, the good record shops, the big brasseries, everything that makes a city vibrate was there, in a quadrilateral between the Jardin des Plantes and Rue du Bac, between the quays and Place Denfert-Rochereau. The Paris events of May 1968 all took place on the Left Bank, and not just around the Sorbonne and the Odéon: the red flag flew everywhere. (Although the great workers' and students' demonstration started from Place de la République, it soon crossed the Seine and ended at Denfert-Rochereau.)

At what point did the Left Bank capsize and become the dreary shop-window it is today? I would place the turning point in the 1970s and 1980s. First of all, the university reform concocted by the dashing Edgar Faure caused the extraordinary concentration of young students in the Latin Quarter to explode to all four corners of the banlieues, after this had made the Latin Quarter lively and cheerful despite the ambient Gaullism. Not all students lived there, but all of them there came to work, to flirt and to drink. Rue Soufflot, Rue des Écoles, the Luxembourg gardens and the Odéon crossroads were their domain. Of course, Jussieu and Censier are still there, but you have to show your identity papers to enter the Sorbonne. The very name of the Latin Quarter has lost its original meaning.

During those years, however, it was the entire heart of the Left Bank that saw its population change. The old psychoanalysts, the old writers, the last proponents of existentialism died, and those who remained were no longer able to pay skyrocketing rents. They were replaced by richer folk for whom culture and art were not a main concern. At the bookshop La Hune, on Boulevard Saint-Germain at the corner with Rue Saint-Benoît (now a Louis Vuitton boutique), you would find a large square table at the entrance where the latest works of philosophy, politics, literary theory and sociology were presented. At a glance, you knew what was going on. But, one day, to my great astonishment, I saw this same table occupied by the latest fashionable novels. The manager explained to me: 'By order of the management. The population of the neighbourhood has changed, you have to show them what they like.' The same logic has affected Tschann, the large bookshop in Montparnasse, which has not flipped over and has courageously maintained its high standards, but at the cost of great difficulties.

In the meantime, the big multiscreen cinemas arrived, changing the very landscape and attracting people from elsewhere in the evenings. And the old historical cafés and restaurants – Le Dôme, La Coupole, La Closerie des Lilas, Les Deux Magots, Le Café de Flore – have become so chic and expensive that the ghosts of Trotsky, Picasso and Sartre would not recognize themselves there.

If I had, despite everything, to recommend a route across the Left Bank, I would choose Rue Saint-Jacques, which has hardly changed since I was a student at the Lycée Louis-le-Grand in the early 1950s. You would start at the bottom, the corner with Quai Saint-Michel, marked by the Hôtel Notre-Dame, where the founding meeting of the COBRA art group (Copenhagen-Brussels-Amsterdam) took place in November 1948. There were some unknowns there who would become famous, including Christian Dotremont, author of the initial manifesto 'La cause était entendue', Asger Jorn, Constant, Corneille...

The walk would finish at the southern end, with the buildings of the Port-Royal maternity hospital, which encompass and hide a church built in the years 1620–50 to replace Port-Royal-des-Champs, the home of Jansenism. As you ascend Rue Saint-Jacques, you would thus have travelled back in time, from modernity to baroque, from Karel Appel to Antoine Le Pautre – a Parisian itinerary on which you would have passed the nave of Saint-Séverin, the church of Saint-Jacques-du-Haut-Pas, the Val de Grâce, and the Scola Cantorum where Erik Satie, Olivier Messiaen and Edgar Varèse studied.

Zinc

What is the most Parisian of all materials? Some would say it is plaster – people say 'plaster of Paris' as they say 'Paris mushrooms', and Balzac speaks of the city on the first page of *Père Goriot* as 'a vale of crumbling stucco watered by streams of black mud'. If Paris did not suffer great fires like the one that destroyed London in 1666, it is very likely thanks to the edict of Philip the Fair that the façades of all houses should be covered with plaster. And most of the poor buildings in the old city were built with half-timbered walls filled with pebbles and plastered. Since then, cinder block and brick, metal and glass have won out everywhere.

But there is one element today that is common to the majority of Parisian buildings: zinc roofing. This appeared under the Restoration and the July Monarchy, became widespread in the Haussmann era and continues to be widely used. Once slightly oxidized, the zinc takes on a bluish-grey hue that blends with the warmer grey, tinged with yellow and a hint of pink, of the plaster used by Arab or Malian masons to coat the façades. Thanks to the know-how of the zinc roofers, the plasticity of zinc makes it possible to surround chimney flues, decorate dormer windows of a sitting-dog shape, wrap the most audacious additions, and use the gutters to emphasize continuity. It can be used for such astonishing achievements as the large, curving attics of the buildings on Place Saint-Michel, housing up to four levels of dwellings. The roofs of Paris, photographed a thousand times and set to song, owe their unity and charm to zinc. And you can find it lower down, on the counters with the day's *Le Parisien*, the little morning coffee, the pastis at apéritif time, the discussions about the latest match of the day. It doesn't matter that the counter is coated with brass (though this does contain zinc), it is indeed *sur le zinc,* despite McDonald's, mobile phones and video games, that a good part of communal life in Paris persists.

Boulevard Périphérique

Since the thirteenth century, five walls have been built around Paris (the walls of Philippe Auguste and Charles V, Louis XIV's boulevard, the Wall of the Farmers-General, the fortifications of Thiers) and one after the other they were destroyed to let the city expand. The Boulevard Périphérique, the last one to date, is still standing despite the question that has gone round and round for more than twenty years: how to get rid of it?

To ask the question in this way is already a wrong approach: assuming that this concrete wall should be dealt with by a single global solution. However, the Périphérique is made up of very different sections. To take the extremes, what is there in common between the western section, nicely buried in the Bois de Boulogne between Porte Maillot and Porte de Saint-Cloud, and the northern section alongside Porte de la Chapelle and Porte de Clignancourt, a hellhole where migrants pitch their tents right alongside the boulevard?

Some people, however, have advocated a comprehensive solution, for example a circular planted promenade, recalling the boulevard built under Louis XIV on the site of Charles V's fortified enclosure. But this reference does not hold: Louis XIV's boulevard really did mark the outer limit of the city. On what are today the '*grands boulevards*', the fine *hôtels* – all on the south side – had a view of the countryside and its dirt roads, with the mills of Butte Montmartre in the distance. The Périphérique, on the other hand, runs almost everywhere through an area long since urbanized, often very densely, and a planted promenade (or a cycle path, or…) would be an artificial patch to hide the problem. We need to get used to the idea that each segment of the Périphérique requires an appropriate treatment.

There are two prerequisites to getting rid of the concrete boulevard. The first is to eliminate car traffic altogether – otherwise we might as well save a few billion and rest content with some one-off improvements. The second is to take advantage of this work to deal with the way that the Périphérique separates Paris from the surrounding municipalities. In this way, we would remain faithful to the spirit of this city, which has always grown in concentric layers rather than pushing out pseudopods or developing metastases like Tokyo or London. The new Greater Paris would be coherent, whereas the plans currently being drawn up, based on centrifugal transport lines, would only further dislocate the urban fabric. I leave aside the fearful problems of property speculation, rising rents, and the expulsion of the poor ever further from the city centre. But the very decision to get rid of the Périphérique presupposes that, in the meantime, the political landscape of the country will have changed sufficiently to prevent these devastating effects.

It will therefore be necessary to urbanize the space between the Boulevards des Maréchaux* and the concrete boulevard, a space that includes the HBM belt of the 1920s. Admittedly, sometimes the Boulevards des Maréchaux and the Périphérique are quite distant from each other (along Boulevard Mortier for example) or separated by a major building (the Robert Debré hospital along Boulevard Sérurier or the defence ministry buildings along Boulevard Victor), and, in this case, it is impossible to treat the area as a whole. But, on the whole, the two boulevards run parallel and close together, and there is everything to be gained by considering the ensemble they form together with the HBMs between them.

More often than not, burying the Périphérique would be insufficient, as shown by the current state of Porte des Lilas, opposite Boulevard Sérurier and Boulevard Mortier. There,

---

* The boulevards that replaced the former city walls, now just inside the Périphérique, are each named after a *maréchal de France* – the highest military distinction. – Translator.

the Périphérique has been hidden underground, leaving a large gap between the outermost HBMs and the first buildings in the communes of Les Lilas and Bagnolet. In an attempt to fill it, a 'green space' was created on the left, the Serge Gainsbourg garden – a lawn surrounded by dusty trees and metal fencing. On the right, a huge cinema was constructed, an all-black cubic block, backing on to a bus depot. None of this connects the top of Rue de Belleville with the first buildings of Les Lilas. There is still a gap of several hundred metres, which is difficult to cross on foot or by bicycle, especially at night.

Not far from here, in contrast, one ensemble stands out against the disaster in the north-east. Based on an idea by Rem Koolhaas, along Boulevard Macdonald the Calberson warehouses dating from the 1960s have been preserved as the foundation for a series of modules designed by fifteen architects. These are joined but their designs and colours are different; some are offices, others housing. From here, crossing Boulevard Macdonald, you enter a small neighbourhood that extends to the Périphérique. Yes, a real neighbourhood, with streets that are not icy corridors as in the new thirteenth arrondissement, with local spots, a school, a cinema – the architecture may be debatable, but the boulevard is enlivened by cafés, restaurants and even a second-hand bookshop. After crossing this neighbourhood, you reach the Périphérique lined with trees and spanned by a wooden pedestrian bridge which allows you to reach Aubervilliers. All that would be needed here to join Paris with the neighbouring commune would be the end of the Périphérique.

The difficulties in making this connection vary from one segment to another. It is not just a question of distance: on a map, between Porte d'Orléans and Porte de Sèvres the Boulevards des Maréchaux and the Périphérique run parallel and very close, but, on the ground, there is a clear difference each side of Porte de Vanves. In one segment, between Porte d'Orléans and Porte de Vanves, Boulevard Brune is bordered by magnificent HBMs from the early 1920s that form a thick belt of brick and stone (or concrete). Opposite, on the

Montrouge side, is a pretty banlieue, with small houses, buildings that were formerly industrial, and a secondary school (College Robert Doisneau, as is only fitting here). In between, the few hundred metres separating Paris from Montrouge are occupied by nice gardens, the Montrouge municipal cemetery and of course, on the Montrouge side, the entrenched Périphérique lined with an anti-noise barrier. Here, it would be enough to fill in this trench and destroy the wall to be able to walk peacefully between Montrouge and Paris. In the other segment, beyond Porte de Vanves, things get more complicated: the belt of HBMs is bisected by blocks dating from the 1960s; the space between Paris and the banlieue (Malakoff) is occupied by huge sports facilities and school buildings (Raspail, François Villon) which it is obviously impossible to remove. The railway tracks of the Montparnasse railway station cross the area overhead, and it ends up with the mass of the Parc des Expositions at Porte de Versailles. The urban space is dislocated and the concealment of the Périphérique (underground in places) would not change much. This contrast between two contiguous segments underlines the need to think about a different solution for each part of the Périphérique.

The infernal ensemble of Porte de la Chapelle could be kept as it is to show Parisians of the future what they have escaped from with the disappearance of the Périphérique.

Street Names

To get from Place de la République to the Canal Saint-Martin, you can choose between Rue Beaurepaire and Rue Léon-Jouhaux. Nicolas Beaurepaire, who commanded the Maine-et-Loire regiment during the Revolution, led the defence of Verdun under siege by the Prussians in September 1792. When the town council decided to capitulate, Beaurepaire shot himself in the head. The Convention voted to transfer his remains to the Panthéon. Léon Jouhaux, for his part, used American money to organize the splitting of the French trade-union movement at the time of the great insurrectionary strikes of 1947. Four years later, he was awarded the Nobel Peace Prize. Thus, at the whim of municipal majorities and the spirit of the times, glory and infamy are neighbours on the blue Paris street signs.

This was not always the case. For a very long time, these streets had names with nothing political about them. Rue des Lavandières Sainte-Opportune, Rue Gît-le-Cœur, Rue du Chat-qui-Pêche, Rue des Blancs-Manteaux: these poetic names were linked to a particular character or detail of the street. They were there to designate, not to honour anyone. The rare exceptions were the names of members of the royal family – such as Place and Rue Dauphine, in honour of the dauphin, the future Louis XIII – or great ministers such as Richelieu, Colbert or Mazarin, but in such cases the name of the street was linked to an *hôtel* that these illustrious figures had built there.

Often, a street would be designated by a visual sign – Rues du Roi Doré, de la Lune, de la Colombe, de l'Arbre-Sec. Elsewhere, it was a local owner such as Julien Lacroix, Aubry-le-Boucher or Bertin-Poirée. Sometimes, the name evoked the trade that was practised there: Ferronnerie, Verrerie, Coutellerie or Grande-Truanderie.* Sometimes it came from a church or convent that the street ran alongside or served: Rue des Nonnains-d'Hyères, Rue des Haudriettes, Rue des Prêtres-Saint-Séverin, or Rue Saint-Martin which led to the large priory of Saint-Martin des Champs, now the Conservatoire des Arts et Métiers.

The Revolution abolished the 'Saints' and rechristened streets of the Ancien Régime that were too inappropriate: Rue Notre-Dame-des-Victoires thus became Rue des Victoires-Nationales, Place Vendôme became Place des Piques, Rue Royale became Rue de la Révolution and Rue des Francs-Bourgeois became Rue des Francs-Citoyens. But the only individuals in the ephemeral revolutionary toponymy were the great martyrs: Place Chalier (de la Sorbonne) and Rue Marat (de l'Ecole-de-Médecine).

It was under the Empire that street names were used for the first time to glorify the regime: the victories – Lodi, Castiglione, Marengo, Rivoli, Austerlitz, Iéna – and the deaths in battle – Desaix (killed at Marengo), Bourdon, Castex, Morland, Valhubert (killed at Austerlitz). Napoleon III would follow his uncle's example: several of Haussmann's new routes bear the name of victories in the Crimea – Alma, Malakoff, Sébastopol – or over the Austrians in Italy – Magenta, Solférino, Palestro, Turbigo. And even the disastrous Mexican adventure has its own street (a reader pointed this out to me), Rue du Borrégo, in the twentieth arrondissement, which immortalizes one of the rare French victories in this sad episode.

With the beginning of the Third Republic, many new names had to be found, both in the central districts where Haussmann's avenues were still under construction, and on the outskirts with the annexation of the 'villages of the crown', from Auteuil to Montmartre, Batignolles to Belleville. The list

---

* Respectively ironmongery, glassmaking, cutlery and villainy. – Translator.

of these names shows the struggle between anticlerical, radical and socialist town councils and the prefect of the Seine, who followed the instructions of the minister of the interior. There is, however, one point on which there seems to have been a consensus: glorification of the colonial epic, in Algeria (Rues de la Smala, de la Mouzaïa, de Constantine), Tonkin (Rue de Sontay) and even China (Rue de Pali-Kao), not to mention the many officers who had earned promotion and decoration in these campaigns, such as Bugeaud, Lamoricière, Lamy, March-and, Gouraud, Mangin, Faidherbe, etc.

Anticlericals and Dreyfusards succeeded in giving Rue des Rosiers, ascending towards the Sacré-Coeur under construction, the name of the Chevalier de la Barre, who was broken on the wheel in 1766 for blasphemy and disrespect towards a religious procession. Similarly, the name of Étienne Dolet, a humanist printer burned in 1546 for spreading atheism, was given to a small street leading to the church of Ménilmontant. The elected representatives of the left even managed to have some of the figures of the Commune celebrated, with Rues Charles-Delescluze, Eugène-Varlin, Jules-Vallès, Jean-Baptiste-Clément and Place Jules-Joffrin.

But the audacity of the councillors had its limits. As far as the Revolution was concerned, they chose to honour Dantonists – Camille Desmoulins, Fabre d'Églantine, Héraut de Séchelles and Danton himself – and Girondins, such as Vergniaud, Pétion or Condorcet. You can even find in the rich districts streets that commemorate presentable Thermidorians such as Cambon or Boissy d'Anglas. But it is not in Paris itself, only in the banlieues, the former red belt, that you have Rues Marat, Robespierre, Varlet or Babeuf. There is indeed a Rue Saint-Just in Paris, but it is hard to find, wedged between the back of the Lycée Honoré-de-Balzac and the Périphérique: nobody lives there, as it runs along the entrance wall of the Batignolles cemetery.

After the Liberation, the socialist-communist municipal council named several major thoroughfares after the dead of the Resistance: Corentin Cariou and Corentin Celton, Marx

Dormoy, Jean-Pierre Timbaud shot at Chateaubriand, Colonel Fabien killed on the Alsace front in 1945, Léon-Maurice Nordmann of the Musée de l'Homme network. There is even a communist woman in this list, Danielle Casanova. In the wake of this, the council decided in 1946 to give the name Place Robespierre to Place du Marché-Saint-Honoré – the site of the Jacobins convent and the famous club of which Robespierre was the leader and most prominent speaker. The anomaly lasted only four years: in 1950, the town council, now in the hands of the right, removed this hated name from the Paris map.

More recently, the construction of a new district around the Bilbiothèque Nationale provided an exceptional opportunity to honour modern literature. But the names chosen are indicative of the literary tastes of our city fathers: not Sartre, Genet, Beckett or Foucault, but François Mauriac, Jean Anouilh, Georges Duhamel and Marguerite Duras.

Today, there are few new streets to be named, and names are given instead to mere crossroads: Place Hannah-Arendt and Place Henri-Krasucki in Belleville, Place Michel-Debré in Saint-Germain-des-Prés. But we could do better: why not rename places whose name is an urban disgrace: Place Napoléon III in front of the Gare du Nord, Avenue Mac Mahon – capitulationist general, factious president, notorious cretin – Rue Thiers, which you might think was impossible in Paris, or Rue Alexis-Carrel, bogus scientist, eugenicist and -Vichyite? And, among the seventy-one generals who have a street named after them, how many were criminals of colonial wars, how many butchers of the people of Paris, whom it would be better to leave anonymous? They could be replaced by women, almost absent from the Paris street plan except for saints and nuns. We could add characters from novels: Lucien de Rubempré or Charles Swann are probably more entitled to have a street named after them in Paris than many old bourgeois and academic glories.

Cafés

In Paris you can rapidly quench a sudden thirst. At any time of the day, even late at night, you are sure to find a bistro, a bar, a café without going very far. Unless you have wandered into one of the few neighbourhoods deprived in this respect, around the government buildings or on one of the long deserted avenues of the sixteenth arrondissement. This is a notable difference from New York, Berlin or London, where the pub, a magnificent institution, involves a certain ceremony, a slow process that has nothing to do with the little black coffee quickly consumed on the counter.

Because what defines a real café is the existence of a counter. Establishments that lack one – whether they never had one or, worse, removed it – can claim the name café but don't deserve it. At the Café de la Paix on Place de l'Opéra, Chez Francis on Place de l'Alma or Les Deux Magots on Place Saint Germain des-Prés, you can certainly order a coffee, but the absence of a counter (as well as the style of the waiters) makes it impossible to confuse it with a real Parisian café.

Over the last dozen years or so, there has been a change in the ordinary café, the place where mothers returning from the crèche meet in the morning and friends meet for an apéritif in the evening. Previously, this would often have been an establishment run by a Kabyle owner who served all by himself – at the bar, in the saloon, or on the terrace if there was one. Sometimes he was assisted by a young man, a recently arrived cousin, but the owner was more Parisian, more 'from the neighbourhood' than many natives of the capital. There are still many such cafés, especially in working-class districts and the banlieues, but, in the city centre, they are increasingly rare. What we find today are cafés that do not limit themselves to '*la limonade*' (the word used in the trade to designate the serving of drinks) but also offer cooked dishes at lunchtime. That's certainly better than being overwhelmed by chains such as McDonald or Subway, but the drawback is that, from 11 o'clock onwards, the tables are set – napkins and cutlery – and it is not always easy to find a table just for a coffee. The most pleasant establishments reserve a few in the corner. Bottles of apéritifs or *digestifs* dating from the 1930s, Suze, Picon, Lillet, Fernet Branca – the usual décor – are still there behind the counter, but the view is blurred by the display of '*formules*' – a word which has replaced the old '*menu*' – and the indication of 'Happy Hours' where the price of a pint of beer is reduced (an English measure formerly unknown in Paris cafés). In Milan or Rome, where coffee and food are better than in Paris, the boundary is maintained between places where you savour a bitter drink standing up, possibly eating a hard-boiled egg, and the trattoria that serves lunch.

Some Paris cafés are said to be 'trendy', without the word being clearly defined. These are not the most chic; the level of elegance is not an issue here. What makes a café trendy is not the décor or the price of drinks, but the clientele. Until recently, there was a textbook case where Rue Desnoyers joins Rue de Belleville: two cafés facing each other. On the left Aux Folies still stands, a café that has been very trendy for at least fifteen years, where the customers are almost all under thirty and mostly white, which makes a striking contrast in one of the most multicoloured streets in Paris. Among them are young men and women without jobs, others who earn their living in a more or less artistic profession – design, architecture, cinema, photography – others again who are foreigners, mostly Americans, living in the neighbourhood or passing through. The few Blacks and Arabs are scattered, rarely in groups, and Chinese are rare in this establishment established in the heart of Chinatown, which has long occupied the lower part of Rue de Belleville. The drink is almost exclusively beer, and the people in groups: it is rare to see an isolated person reading the newspaper in a corner. Both sexes are dressed, coiffed and shod in a very coded way, varying according to the seasons, which makes for a homogeneous population whose members bear a striking resemblance to one another. To a benevolent eye, this is a group of young people having fun together; alternatively, it is an assembly of clones that can be found with a few variations in all the cafés of the same kind.

Opposite, the Vieux Saumur was (in the past tense, because it was demolished when the adjoining segment of Rue Desnoyers was destroyed by the Paris town hall) an old-fashioned café: fewer people, less noise, old people from the neighbourhood, Arab workers, isolated customers or couples. Encounters there were peaceful, you could read quietly and even write. There might have been a jukebox or a pinball machine there, just like in the old days. It was a haven like many that still exist today – for as long as they last.

Trendy cafés don't spring up just anywhere. They proliferate in working-class neighbourhoods (with a high population of immigrant origin) that are in the process of gentrification. There is often an initial trigger – for example, the Café-Charbon on Rue Oberkampf, an old shop transformed in the 1990s, which launched 'trendiness' in its street and the surrounding micro neighbourhood. Areas around markets, where the population is more mixed than elsewhere, are also conducive to the blossoming of trendy cafés, as in Aligre or the Kurdish stronghold at the beginning of Rue du Faubourg Saint-Denis, or more recently around the pretty Marché de l'Olive in the north of the eighteenth arrondissement.

The Parisian café has long been a literary and artistic setting. For Diderot and Balzac, Breton and Miller, Manet and Brassaï, the café was much more than just a backdrop: it illuminated its denizens' physique and soul. Groups were founded in cafés, such as COBRA in 1948 in the café of the Hôtel Notre-Dame, on the corner of Rue Saint-Jacques and Quai Saint-Michel. For the surrealists and the Situationist International, the rhythms of their lives were marked by encounters in cafés. And then, around the time the laptop appeared (without any clear causal link), this tropism, whose origins go back to the literary cafés of the nineteenth century, unravelled. This is why one can take comfort from reading in Yannick Haenel's *Tiens ferme ta couronne* a long passage that takes place in a café called Les Petits Oignons, whose walls are painted red and which is located in the twentieth arrondissement not far from Place Gambetta.

Végétalisation

The word is not pretty, but the reality is worse. It's taking a place that's not bothering anyone and disfiguring it. Example: Square Bolivar, a sloping triangle between the boulevard of that name and Rue Clavel, had a surface of large irregular paving stones and five superb chestnut trees aligned on the median of the triangle. The *végétaliseurs* struck a few years ago. Now, the paved area is divided by cement blocks, and the chestnut trees trapped inside a metal fence. The dark green triangle has had soil poured in and been planted with the dull and dusty shrubs that the managers of green spaces are so fond of. A place worthy of being photographed by Cartier-Bresson or Robert Frank has been transformed into a fragment of a new town parachuted into the heart of the nineteenth arrondissement. The same fencing and shrubs can be found all along Boulevard de la Villette, as well as on the noble curve of Boulevard de Rochechouart and Boulevard de Clichy. During the First World War, Sacha Guitry made a series of short films entitled *Ceux de chez nous*. In one of these films, we see an elderly man walking slowly through the crowd on Boulevard de Clichy. Guitry's off-screen comment: 'It's Degas.' How could a nearly blind painter find his way through the fences, cycle paths and metal barriers – all the jumble that now clutters the boulevard?

There is worse yet. All over the city, the decorative fences surrounding and protecting the feet of trees have been removed. Instead, 'green spaces' have been created, a few square metres of scrappy grass that soon gets sprinkled with empty cans and greasy paper. On Boulevard de Belleville, between these 'green spaces' are brightly coloured benches and fitness equipment that is completely out of place. It would be hard to find a better way to ignore or despise the spirit of a place. In his introduction to *Les promenades de Paris,* Alphand, the great architect-gardener responsible for so many Paris public gardens, wrote: 'The artist's thought is guided by general formulae, transmitted by tradition and modified by everyday demands, which together give all the works of an era and a nation a particular physiognomy, in harmony with the degree of civilization that a people has attained, and that characterizes its spirit.' To what degree of civilization have we then fallen?

Jean-Paul Sartre

Ten years ago, we published at La Fabrique a book by the English writer Ian Birchall, *Sartre Against Stalinism*. An excellent work that covers some fifty years of Sartre's political trajectory and describes what the non-communist far left then was, its leading figures – Colette Audry, David Rousset, Merleau-Ponty, Daniel Guérin, Claude Lefort and many others – and its struggles during the Cold War, the Algerian War, the Vietnam War, the events of May 68. I praised the book to Natacha, a bookseller whose opinions counted a lot for me and still do. She told me, 'It won't sell' and to my astonishment she added, 'No one is interested in Sartre these days.' She was right, the book was a complete flop.

How is such forgetfulness possible? Have we forgotten how Sartre was at the forefront of all the good fights of his time? Let's recall them in case anyone forgets – I'm relying on the excellent biography of Annie Cohen-Solal. In 1952, Sartre published *Saint Genet, Actor and Martyr*, a long portrait, a long apologia, for a convicted criminal, a thief and – worse still – a guy who boasted of being a homosexual (today's word, people still said *pédéraste* at that time). A huge scandal, Mauriac and Claudel were horrified, but people forget that, at this time, homosexuality was equally frowned upon on the left, among the communists and even the surrealists. The same year, Sartre gave his support to Henri Martin, a sailor and communist, imprisoned for his action against the war in Indochina, publishing a long text in a collective work with Jean-Marie Domenach, Michel Leiris and Jacques Prévert. 'It's his Calas affair,'* people said at the time. During the

---

* In 1762, Voltaire published a celebrated vindication of the Protestant Jean Calas, executed for 'heresy'. – Translator.

Algerian war, Sartre defended Francis Jeanson, head of a support network in France for the FLN; he testified at Jeanson's trial and contributed to 'Manifesto of the 121' which he published in full in his magazine, *Les Temps modernes*. Thierry Maulnier wrote in *Le Figaro* of 30 September 1960: 'Real France must be defeated for Sartre's France to triumph, the revolutionary idea of France which Monsieur Jean-Paul Sartre has substituted for France, which he prefers to France.' On the Champs-Élysées, people shouted '*Algérie française*' and '*Fusillez Sartre!*' In 1961, he wrote a resounding preface to Frantz Fanon's *The Wretched of the Earth*, published by Maspero. His flat on Rue de Rennes was bombed in 1962. He refused the Nobel Prize awarded to him in 1964. In 1968, he chaired the Russell Tribunal which investigated the war crimes of the US army in Vietnam. During the May events, he declared his solidarity with the students – who called him 'Polo' – and spoke on 20 May in the main amphitheatre of the occupied Sorbonne – the only intellectual who could speak in public during these hot weeks.

In May 1970, Sartre agreed to become managing director of *La Cause du peuple*, a Maoist newspaper regularly seized by the forces of interior minister Marcellin. Together with Simone de Beauvoir, he went out selling the paper on the main boulevards and was even detained for a few hours. On 21 October 1970, he spoke to workers leaving the Renault factory in Billancourt – a famous image of this little man in his anorak standing on an oil drum, microphone in hand. In May 1973, with Serge July and Philippe Gavi, he founded the newspaper *Libération*. 'For six months I'm abandoning literature and philosophy, I want people to see that I've done everything I could for this paper.' In December 1974, very ill and almost blind, he managed to visit Andreas Baader, on hunger strike in the Stammheim prison near Stuttgart. At a press conference he declared: 'The living conditions in this prison are intolerable. The government and the prison authorities have a peculiar way of dealing with political prisoners.'

An impressive journey, a wonderful life – not to mention

his output as philosopher, novelist and playwright. How can we explain the current disfavour?

I can think of four reasons for this, developed in different milieus. Among specialists, Sartre's philosophy is no longer much in vogue. For him, the notion of subject was crucial, but structuralism first of all, and then authors as influential as Michel Foucault and Gilles Deleuze, relegated the subject to the back burner. For the far left, his rapprochement with a PCF that was ever more Stalinist (a four-year flirtation, from the demonstration against Ridgway in 1952 to the Soviet intervention in Hungary in 1956) was an inexcusable mistake. For almost everyone, Sartre was wrong in his controversy with Camus; few people know the details, but Camus today is a French idol that there can be no question of debunking. Finally, and more recently, Houria Bouteldja, an eminent member of the Indigènes de la République, in a book that has earned our publishing house many enemies, especially among those who have not read it (*Les Blancs, les Juifs et nous*, La Fabrique 2016), criticized Sartre for his loyalty to the Zionist project, his 'good white conscience'.

There is surely some truth in all these complaints, but one point brings me closer to him, making me one of Sartre's orphans: he was a Parisian. Not a *Parisian writer* – unless I am mistaken he never wrote about Paris, although his great novel in three volumes, *The Roads to Freedom*, has Paris as its backdrop. But he can be posthumously awarded the title of honorary Parisian. All his life was spent in Paris, apart from the interlude of war. Always on the Left Bank. On his release from Germany, he lived with Simone de Beauvoir at the Hôtel Louisiane, Rue de Seine. In 1945, he moved (with his mother) to 42 Rue Bonaparte, opposite the church of Saint-Germain-des-Prés, where he stayed for seventeen years. In 1962, he left Saint-Germain for Montparnasse and took a small studio on Boulevard Raspail, which he was forced to leave in 1974 for an ugly building on Boulevard Edgar Quinet. Some cafés – Le Raspail Vert on Boulevard Raspail, La Liberté at the corner of Boulevard Edgar Quinet and Rue de la Gaîté, where he took breakfast and smoked his first cigarettes of the day – are, for me (and no doubt for others), places of memory.

One day, in the 1970s, I saw Sartre sitting, tired, on a bench in Place Saint-Sulpice. Simone de Beauvoir was standing next to him. It was moving and I felt like going to embrace them or doing what Léautaud recounts in his *Journal*, when he sent a child to take a bouquet of violets to Verlaine, who was drinking his wine, slumped in a café at the bottom of Rue Soufflot. But there was no child and no violets, and, in the end, I did nothing, for which I still reproach myself to this day.

Urban Eyesores

Rue Lesage is a short street between Rue Julien-Lacroix and Rue Tourtille. Like most of the streets in the neighbourhood, it is lined with three- or four-storey buildings dating from the second half of the nineteenth century, working-class housing made homogeneous by its fine pale-yellow plaster, a Paris tradition maintained by successive generations of masons, from Italians to Portuguese, and Malians today. In the middle of the street, on the left-hand side as you go uphill, the charm is broken by a block that is almost square, in a smooth dark grey, which stands out from the discreet harmony of the street by its brutal shape and horrible colour.

On Rue de Belleville there stood until recently a dilapidated building that could have been perfectly well repaired. Instead, it was demolished and a new construction put in its place, whose lines and apertures have nothing in common with the adjacent buildings. This eyesore is covered with a synthetic material of a glaring whiteness that contrasts with the soft colour of the street. Violence has been done to the respectable old lady that is Rue de Belleville by imposing this hideous foreign body.

Aberrations of this kind are the work of architects who probably never came to the site, simply using computer designs with no heed for the proposed location. And these scandals remain anonymous. I would propose that, as in the past, the names of the architect and, still more important, the person who signed the building permit, be indicated, names that deserve to be pilloried for a long time to come.

Art Nouveau

Art Nouveau in Paris pales by comparison with its dazzling blossoming in capitals such as Brussels, Vienna and Munich. In France, it was not well received, coming from a Germanic world, relations with which were marked at the time by mistrust if not hostility. French institutional architects of the early twentieth century remained faithful to the eclecticism and teaching of Viollet-le-Duc. The major buildings presented in the few books on Art Nouveau in Paris – the Samaritaine department store, the church of Saint-Jean de Montmartre – were certainly innovations, but they retain a neoclassical stiffness, lacking the curved line and floral decoration that mark the art of Otto Wagner or Victor Horta.

It may be objected that there are nuggets of Art Nouveau scattered right across Paris, so familiar that they are not looked at with all the attention they deserve: these are the Métro entrances designed by Hector Guimard from 1900 to 1913. The most common form is a cast-iron balustrade rounded at the corners and decorated with floral emblems whose stem forms a small M barely visible in the midst of the petals. The finest example is the entrance portico formed by two long metallic curves that extend in several arches: one facing outward, bearing at its far end one of the two orange lamps that make the entrance to the Métro visible at night; the other facing inward, ending in a panel where the word '*Métropolitain*' is inscribed in an Art Nouveau typography designed by Guimard himself. On the balustrade, another larger panel bears the name of the station and a map of the Métro, all illuminated by a lamp with a floral motif.

Guimard also designed other entrances, small buildings covered with a gabled roof extended by a fan-shaped canopy. Two examples remain, one at the Abbesses station, the other at the exit from Châtelet on Place Sainte-Opportune.

Of the 167 Métro entrances designed by Guimard, 87 remain. The others have been demolished and replaced by metalwork that looks like something dreamed up by designers from the prison administration. An exception however is the entrance to the Raspail station, which was dismantled and reconstructed in New York for the collection of the Museum of Modern Art. The attention paid to Guimard's Métro entrances should encourage people to go and admire the wonders he built in the sixteenth arrondissement, including Castel Béranger and his own home on Avenue Mozart.

Studded Crossings

Pedestrian crossings were not always marked by white or yellow stripes painted on the roadway. Twenty or thirty years ago, pedestrians walked between two parallel rows of large round-headed studs driven into the asphalt every fifty centimetres or so: these were the *passages cloutés*. The thing has disappeared, but there is still a trace of it in everyday language: to say of someone that he is '*dans les clous*' means that he is in order, complying with the various legal injunctions we are deluged with.

Places

Unlike Rome, Paris is not a city of squares; while many Paris *places* bear the name, there are few that deserve it. A real *place* is a space that, if not enclosed, is at least provided with a continuous outline. If there is a gaping hole on one side, the '*place* effect' disappears. The Châtelet could be a real *place*, and quite beautiful with the two theatres facing each other and the quay, with Tour de l'Horloge and the mass of the Palais de Justice behind. But the fourth side was ripped open by the construction of Boulevard de Sébastopol, Rue Saint-Denis and the unfortunate Avenue Victoria, and the meagre Chambre des Notaires is not enough to fill the void. So, the Châtelet is a failed *place*, or rather simply a crossroads of the main Paris traffic routes.

Another element that constitutes a real *place* is animation – not mainly car traffic, but the presence of cafés, restaurants, bakeries, in short, something other than luxury fashion shops. The most famous Paris *places*, Concorde, Étoile and Bastille are great roundabouts where cars dodge each other the best they can and the pedestrian is constantly endangered. What they lack most to be real *places* is precisely human life. The Campo dei Fiori in Rome is a *place* where you can meet up with friends, have a drink, buy vegetables and flowers, where you feel good. Who could think of meeting someone on Place de la Concorde or drinking a coffee on Place de l'Étoile?

There are, however, some real *places* in Paris. The oldest and most venerable is Place Maubert (after Master Albert, a thirteenth-century philosopher), which itself dates from the Middle Ages. During the Wars of Religion, this was where Protestants were tortured and burned, as well as 'heretics' such as the humanist printer Étienne Dolet, strangled and burned in 1546 at the age of 37. There used to be a bronze statue of Dolet here, of which André Breton wrote in *Nadja* that it 'always attracted him and caused him unbearable discomfort'. The statue was melted down during the Occupation, but there is a Rue Étienne Dolet which rises from Boulevard de Ménilmontant towards the Ménilmontant church.

Place Maubert is crossed by Boulevard Saint-Germain; you could even say it is shaped by it, formed by a widening of the boulevard which slows and dilates here like a large river flowing into a lake. The pavements on the south side (towards the Panthéon) are occupied twice a week by a market – a real market, as in Aligre or Belleville, not a fake market where the stalls are just an extension of regular shops onto the pavement, such as on Rue de Seine or Rue Montorgueil. Opposite, on the Rue de Bièvre side, you go down two or three steps – a difference which makes for much of the *place*'s character – to reach an old-established and delicious Vietnamese restaurant and a Japanese grocery shop. From there, crossing Rue Monge, you come across a café, Le Maubert, facing south-east and pleasant at the beginning of spring.

Place Maubert has a remarkable title of nobility. During the uprising of supporters of the Duc de Guise in 1588, which led to the expulsion of Henri III from his capital, this was the site of the first of all those barricades that were to punctuate the life of the city for centuries.

Place des Vosges, somewhat more recent, is also a real *place*, of Italian influence, supervised by the architects who arrived with Marie de Médicis, hence the covered arcades. It was originally paved and empty. A garden was then planted, enclosed by metal gates, in the middle of which Louis XIII sits enthroned. Place Dauphine, which also dates from the time of Henri IV, was probably a marvel before the base of its triangle was demolished to make way for the awful rear façade of the Palais de Justice – and before an underground car park raised the ground level. Are Place des Victoires and Place Vendôme, built under Louis XIV, real *places*? From an architectural point of view, yes, without a doubt. But human life? There are only luxury shops (the very word 'shop' sounds strange for these displays of dresses, watches and jewellery at extravagant prices, with a guard at the entrance, certainly needed). Not a café, though there is the Ritz bar, but you have to wear a tie.

What remains are the *places* developed on the site of the former barriers of the Wall of the Farmers-General. Some of them are irremediable, such as the ugly and noisy Place d'Italie. Others are lively, animated and popular: on the Left Bank, Place Denfert-Rochereau; on the Right Bank, Place Clichy, Place Stalingrad, the Belleville crossroads where four Parisian arrondissements meet and which concentrates their charm; the Ménilmontant crossroads where the curve of the boulevard is like a rough outline of a square, Place de la Nation with Dalou's *Triumph of the Republic*, which, even in the midst of the motorized whirl and recently planted bushes, gives the *place* its nobility and makes it the destination for countless demonstrations.

A word should also be said about the many triangles formed by the divergence of two streets. They obviously do not deserve the name of *place*, but they often have the charm described by Walter Benjamin in his *Arcades Project* (I have already quoted this passage in *The Invention of Paris*, but I cannot resist the temptation):

> the little timeless squares that suddenly are there, and to which no name attaches. They have not been the object of careful planning, like the Place Vendôme or the Place de Grève, and do not enjoy the patronage of world history, but owe their existence to houses that have slowly, sleepily, belatedly assembled in response to the summons of the century. In such squares, the trees hold sway; even the smallest afford thick shade. Later, however, in the gaslight, their leaves have the appearance of dark-green frosted glass near the street lamps, and their earliest green glow at dusk is the automatic signal for the start of spring in the big city.*

* Walter Benjamin, *The Arcades Project* (Cambridge, MA: Belknap Press, 2002), p. 516.

Île de la Cité

The Île de la Cité is a horror, the worst failure of Haussmann and those who followed him. Moreover, the baron hated this place, which he was obliged to cross every morning to go to the faculty of law, as he says in his *Mémoires*: 'the sorry huddle of low dives that then dishonoured the Île de la Cité, which I would have the joy of razing completely – a haunt of thieves and murderers, who seemed able there to brave the correctional police and the court of assizes'. Haussmann worked to empty the Cité of its homeless population and destroy its stinking and dangerous alleyways. The result: Parisians cross the Cité without stopping, between the walls of the Préfecture de Police and the walls of the Hôtel-Dieu, or through the gloomy Rue d'Arcole full of tatty souvenir shops. One of François Hollande's last misdeeds was to entrust the renovation of the island to Dominique Perrault, responsible for the Grande Bibliothèque, where the books are in towers and the readers in cellars. And the big question is whether the spire of Notre-Dame will be rebuilt identically or not.

I have a proposal to restore to the Cité, if not its ancient splendour (the seventeen churches that have disappeared will not be rebuilt), at least something of its former spirit. We would start by destroying the Préfecture de Police, an ugly building full of bad memories. We would also destroy the Hôtel-Dieu, ugly and inconvenient like almost all the Paris hospitals of the nineteenth century. This would create a large open space between the two arms of the Seine, from the Palais de Justice to the façade of Notre-Dame. This space could then be entirely rebuilt, without leaving a forecourt in front of the cathedral, which is not meant to be seen from hundreds of metres away: all medieval cathedrals were designed to be admired with your nose in the air. Who should be entrusted with this reconstruction? Above all, not fashionable architects, Nouvel and others. We could put people to work who know the trade, workers from the banlieues and elsewhere, and give free rein to popular inventiveness, guided by modest architects respectful of the ideas of others (there are such). It would be a new neighbourhood, with streets, cafés, bakeries, libraries and cinemas, which architects and tourists from all over the world would come to admire. Quasimodo, Esmeralda, the Chourineur and Rodolphe would feel at ease there if they returned, and Parisians would rediscover their Cité, today occupied by sword, cassock and scalpel.

Surrealism

I'm drinking a beer at a village café in Provence and, for some reason, I don't know why, I think of Surrealism. At the next table are some young people, three boys and a girl, intelligent looking. I ask them – if I say Surrealism, what does it conjure up? Almost in one voice they answer: 'Dali.' I insist a little: not Breton, not Duchamp, not Buñuel? 'No, Dali – he's close to us, he could make himself understood; with the others, it's complicated.'

So, this movement, which for many years shook the world from Czechoslovakia to Mexico, has left nothing behind for young people except Dali, in other words, nothing. One possible reason for this is that, in Paris, where the movement was born and existed for thirty or forty years, there are no vestiges left – no material traces to feed the imagination, such as Victor Hugo's house or the statue of Balzac. It is as if it never existed. Some devotees mentally raise their hats as they pass 42 Rue Fontaine, but there is nothing left to see there, Breton's studio was sold in bits without the state lifting a finger. The Passage de l'Opéra where the movement began was destroyed by the extension of Boulevard Haussmann (the only new cutting of the inter-war period, in every respect detestable), as Aragon recounts in *The Paris Peasant*. The Galerie du Thermomètre and the Galerie du Baromètre, where the surrealists used to meet at the Café Certa, remain only in Marville's photos taken fifty years before their destruction. And the countless cafés where the movement met – the Café Cyrano on Place Blanche, the Café du Globe at Porte Saint-Denis, the Café d'Angleterre at Richelieu-Drouot, the Promenade de Vénus on Rue du Louvre in the 1960s – have either disappeared or changed their names, and the memory of Surrealism has evaporated. The bookshops where some important events took place – for example the Sans Pareil on Avenue Kléber, where the first Max Ernst exhibition in May–June 1921 left all visitors stunned – no longer exist. And the galleries where influential exhibitions were organized, the Galerie Surréaliste on Rue Jacques-Callot, the Galerie Ratton on Rue Laffitte, the Galerie des Beaux-Arts on Rue du Faubourg-Saint-Honoré, the Étoile Scellée on Rue du Pré-aux-Clercs, remain only in our memory.

Another possible reason to explain the answer of those young people is the systematic denigration of André Breton – 'the pope of Surrealism', expeller-in-chief, a moralist who didn't like queers – in short a pain in the arse, and a movement personified by a pain in the arse has nothing to attract young people. It is certainly true that the man was not always congenial, but he could also be welcoming, open, generous. If he fought so hard, if he expelled so many old friends, it was to keep the line that allowed Surrealism to exist for so long, avoiding the mistakes that so many others made. Aragon was expelled (along with Éluard) for joining the Communist Party, and the rest of his career showed how justified this separation was.

One could dream (one can always dream) of a small museum of Surrealism in Paris, where there would be not works of art but photographs telling the history of the movement, showing all its courage and its humour, the friendships made across the world, the rightness of its political positions, everything that makes it still present in our time and even often missed.

The Bourse

At the height of his glory, Napoleon commissioned several great monuments for Paris, the Arc de Triomphe, the Madeleine – which was to be the temple of Victory – and the most original and most modern, the Bourse. Its architect was Alexandre Brongniart, to whom the Parisians also owe the romantic layout of Père-Lachaise. He was a pupil of Étienne Louis Boullée, who was not only a great architect (only one small *hôtel* remains of all his work, on Rue de la Ville-l'Évêque, invisible because it has become the headquarters of the telecom company Free) but, above all, a visionary designer. His Bibliothèque Royale would have housed thousands of readers. For Newton, he imagined a spherical cenotaph with zenithal lighting. 'Oh Newton!' he wrote in his *Essai sur l'Art* (1797). 'If by your great enlightenment and the sublimity of your genius you have determined the face of the Earth, I have conceived the project of enveloping you in your discovery. In a sense, it is a way of wrapping you in yourself.' Brongniart followed Boullée's lectures – as did Chalgrin, architect of the Arc de Triomphe, and Jacques-Nicolas Durand, who taught architecture at the École Polytechnique from its foundation by the Convention until 1840. One could say that the Bourse is the great and unique Boulléen project in Paris. Neo-classical, of course, but not only: its footprint, almost square with four recessed corners, its continuous colonnade along all four sides and corners, its lack of decoration, its massive and compact character are indeed of Boulléan inspiration.

Before the Bourse was completed (1826), the buying and selling of shares took place at various sites in central Paris, warehouses or cafés, as can be read in the passages of *La*

Comédie humaine that take place under the Empire. The opening of the Bourse coincided with the development of the stock market. Its operation at its peak is described by Zola in his novel *Money*, set largely in the Palais Brongniart:

> But the dreadful din became such, amid epileptic gesticulation, that the agents themselves could no longer hear each other. Agitated by their professional fury, they continued with gestures, since the cavernous bass of some failed to carry, while the high register of others thinned to nothing. Enormous mouths opened without a distinct noise emerging from them, and hands alone spoke: an outgoing gesture that offered, an incoming one that accepted. Raised fingers indicated the quantities, heads said yes or no with a sign ... Between the cash desk and the trading floor, above the raging storm of heads, there were only the three quoters, seated on their high chairs, floating like shipwrecks with the large white spots of their registers, dragged left and right by the rapid fluctuations in the quotations thrown at them.

Today, electronics have made all these picturesque phenomena disappear; purchases and sales are made in tiny fractions of a second and the Palais Brongniart is empty. Attempts have been made to establish more or less artistic activities in the building, but they have all come to nothing. Why not turn it into a large central library, like in New York, open to everyone and especially to students? It would be better than the lamentable spectacle of readers lining up to enter the library at the Centre Pompidou. Instead, the more likely outcome is another luxury restaurant, or even a shopping mall. From the Paris town hall, which owns the building, we can only expect the worst.

Parisian Writers

I would suggest confining the title of 'Parisian writer' to those for whom Paris was an essential source of inspiration. Being born in Paris or having lived there all your life does not do the trick – authors like Valéry, Gide or Malraux have all sorts of qualities except for being Parisian writers, even if they may have written books that are set in Paris.

If we accept this definition, we can say that there were no Parisian writers before the nineteenth century: the city in general is not a theme before 1800. Even Diderot, a Parisian at heart, did not write much about Paris – except for the marvellous beginning of *Rameau's Nephew* ('Whether the weather is good or bad, my custom is to go out at 5 o'clock in the afternoon for a walk at the Palais-Royal. It's me you see, always alone, dreaming on the Argenson bench').

In the nineteenth century, then, I see three figures whose work is woven with Parisian thread, three figures who have left their mark on the city in the same way as great stone monuments. They are of course Balzac, Baudelaire and Hugo. They were almost contemporaries and knew one another to varying degrees. Balzac and Hugo were close friends; they used to go for walks together or dine at the Rocher de Cancale. 'Here, my dear Hugo, is the dedication of *Illusions perdues* that I am sending you in proof, I will come and see you next Friday at noon. Warmest greetings.' By dedicating to him what he considered a centrepiece of his work, Balzac shows the level at which he placed his friend. Hugo visited him on his deathbed and delivered the epitaph at his grave. Baudelaire may only have bumped into Balzac at the Hôtel Pimodan ('I saw him once in a meeting where there was talk of the prodigious effects of hashish,' he wrote in *Artificial Paradises*) but his admiration was immense. Balzac was, for him, 'this prodigious meteor that will cover our country with a cloud of glory, like a strange and exceptional orient, a polar dawn flooding the frozen desert with its fairy lights' (from 'Madame Bovary by Gustave Flaubert'). Baudelaire dedicated to Hugo several great poems from *Les Fleurs du mal* ('The Swan', 'The Seven Old Men', 'The Little Old Ladies'), but his judgement was quite varied. He can be more than laudatory ('Thus, in Victor Hugo's poems, these accents of love for fallen women, for poor people crushed in the gears of our societies, for the animal martyrs of our gluttony and despotism, are constantly present. Few people have noticed the charm and enchantment of kindness combined with strength, which is so frequently seen in the works of our poet. A smile and a tear in the face of a colossus is an almost divine originality', in 'L'Art romantique'). But he was sometimes scornful, as in a letter of 3 November 1865 to his mother: 'I would accept neither his glory nor his fortune if I had to possess at the same time his immense ridiculousness ... He tried this time [in *Les Chansons des rues et des bois*] to be joyful and light, to be in love and make himself young again. It's dreadfully heavy. I see in these things, as in so many others, just another opportunity to thank God for not having given me so much foolishness.' In another letter to his mother, he described *Les Misérables* as a 'filthy and inept' book. This oscillation between admiration and annoyance was, moreover, frequent at the time – even with Balzac, who was often annoyed by Hugo's self-assurance.

In *Réflexions sur quelques-uns de mes contemporains*, Baudelaire wrote: 'Victor Hugo has not been with us for many years now. I remember the time when his face was one of the most often encountered among the crowds; and many times I have wondered, seeing him so often appearing in the turbulence of parties or the silence of solitary places, how he could reconcile the necessities of his assiduous work with this sublime, but dangerous, taste for walks and daydreams.' Hugo, then, was a Paris pedestrian – not the most common

image we have of him, which is more one of a solitary man
on his rock. But this leads on to a common feature of Parisian
writers, almost worthy of being part of the definition: they are
walkers in Paris, and solitary walkers – which is why Proust is
not, in my opinion, a Parisian writer, despite his keen ear for
the sounds of Paris. Balzac, for his part, travelled all over the
city in his big boots, between his printers, his publishers, his
mistresses, his coffee merchants. 'For me there are memories
at every door, thoughts at every lamppost. Not a façade has
been built, or a building knocked down, but I have spied on
its birth or death. I take part in the immense movement of this
world as if I had its soul' (in *Le Mendiant*). Baudelaire too
walked endlessly in Paris. After leaving the Île Saint-Louis, he
had neither a desk, a table, nor a notebook to take care of at
home, and he dreamed his verses while walking through the
city, as he expresses it in 'The Sun':

> Along the old street on whose cottages are hung
> The slatted shutters which hide secret lecheries,
> When the cruel sun strikes with increased blows
> The city, the country, the roofs, and the wheat fields,
> I go alone to try fanciful fencing,
> Scenting in every corner the chance of a rhyme,
> Stumbling over words as over paving stones,
> Colliding at times with lines dreamed of long ago.*

Balzac, Hugo and Baudelaire created Parisian types: Rastignac,
Javert, Gavroche. With Baudelaire, they often have no proper
name, simply the Redheaded Beggar, the Passer-by, the
Fanfarlo, the Dandy, but they are always among us, in 'a per-
petual, simultaneous relationship between the ideal and life'.
Although large parts of both *Les Fleurs du mal* and the *Petits
poèmes en prose* are set in Paris, Baudelaire does not give
any address, any indication of a precise place, except in 'The
Swan', clearly located in the former Carrousel neighbourhood.

---

* Charles Baudelaire, *The Flowers of Evil*, trans. William Aggeler
(Fresno, CA, 1964).

(The same indeterminacy can be found in Jean-Luc Godard, whose films up to *La Chinoise* are almost all set in Paris or the inner suburbs, with it rarely being clear in which street or even in which neighbourhood the action takes place.)

For Stendhal, who was a close contemporary of Balzac, Baudelaire and Hugo, things were clear: 'In its physical aspect, I never liked Paris. Even around 1803, I hated it for not having mountains around it ... Today, I value Paris. I confess that for courage it must be placed in the forefront, as also for cooking and for *spirit*. But it doesn't seduce me any the more for that. It seems to me that there is always *comedy* in its virtue.' And then: 'I can hardly find any pleasure from music sung in a French hall' (*Memoirs of an Egotist*). Stendhal is really not a Parisian writer, his city was Milan. That's where he learned to love Mozart, where he understood politics, where he started writing, where he experienced great (unhappy) love. And we know that he asked for the following to be written on his grave: '*Arrigo Beyle, Milanese*'.

Changing Streets

Paris being a living organism, the streets that make it up evolve and sometimes change their role, theme or activity. Some of them, however, retain the imprint of what they once were. About Rue Vivienne, Mercier wrote in his *Tableau de Paris* (1788): 'There is more money in this single street than in all the rest of the city ... The major counting-houses have their offices there, in particular the Caisse d'Escompte. This is the stamping ground of the bankers, the money-changers, the brokers, all who make a trade out of money ... The whores are more financial here than in any other quarter, and never mistaken in marking out a henchman of the Bourse.' Today, Rue Vivienne between the Bourse and Boulevard Montmartre is still the domain of gold. Cheek by jowl are shops where you can buy and sell ingots, napoléons, scraps of gold, Greek, Egyptian, Celtic and Roman coins, ancient medals, louis d'or, American coins dating from the War of Independence, scales for weighing gold. The vendors sit behind reinforced windows, a modern touch in this ancient street.

Another urban continuity: the Passage du Caire, the oldest in Paris (1799), whose name bears witness to the Egyptomania that followed Bonaparte's expedition to the banks of the Nile. It originally specialized in *calicots* – today one would say advertising streamers – for clothing shops. Very soon, these streamers were produced by screen printing, and the printers were called *calicots*. Even today, this arcade still offers material for window displays of clothing – hangers, mannequins, etc. Tourists are rarely interested in this arcade, so that there are no restaurants or trinket shops like in the Passage des Panoramas or the Passage du Choiseul. Let's hope that lasts.

Other streets have lost their distinctive mark over time. For example, Rue du Faubourg-Saint-Antoine, which was long devoted to the manufacture of wooden furniture. Some people think this activity was linked to the proximity of the depots for wood floated down the Seine, the most important of these being on the Île Louviers, since joined to the Right Bank alongside Boulevard Morland (the Chourineur, in Eugène Sue's *Mystères de Paris*, was a worker on this island); others see another reason: the faubourg was the Paris destination for workers from Germany, who were particularly skilled in furniture manufacture. However it may be, the beautiful courtyards that bear such poetic names – Étoile d'Or, Maison-Brûlée, Trois-Frères, Passage de la Main-d'Or, Rue de la Forge-Royale, Passage de la Boule-Blanche, Cour du Bel-Air – were all occupied by workshops where furniture was made. Mercier wrote in the *Tableau de Paris*: 'I do not know how this faubourg survives. Furniture is sold from one end to the other; and the poor population that live here have no furniture at all.' Today there are still a few workshops where wood is worked, but the faubourg is now devoted to very different activities: architecture and design agencies, photographers' workshops, publishing houses, recording studios and the like. There are also many people who have moved here and transformed workshops into lofts. In short, the great working-class faubourg, leader of all the revolutions of the eighteenth and nineteenth centuries and the last to take down the red flag, no longer exists. It has become gentrified.

Conversely, in some streets that had previously been unremarkable, activities have appeared that could not have been foreseen. Rue Mongallet, which gives onto Rue de Reuilly near Place de la Nation, has, in a few years become the street of electronics. All along its length, on both sides, are computers of all brands, new and second-hand, but above all there are countless shiny boxes containing things I can't even imagine ('Mediashare Wireless, Kit including AMD Ryzen processor and ASUS x 570 Prime motherboard', etc.). The non-geek that I am cannot identify a tenth of the contents of the showcases. Why this strange concentration occurred here remains a mystery.

Older and less mysterious is the colonization of Rue de Douai between Rue Fontaine and Rue Pigalle by shops selling guitars of all kinds, acoustic and electric, new and second-hand, luxurious or cheap. There is even a left-handed guitar shop. The reason for this, a shopkeeper explained to me, is that Pigalle being a nightclub district, musicians were particularly numerous. 'It's the same in London and Tokyo, in all the big cities music shops are in the red-light districts.'

One could also mention Rue Keller and its numerous manga shops, or Rue de Marseille and its lines of elegant clothes shops. Contrary to the prevailing *déclinisme*, life in the city continues as much as ever.

Bobos

The Parisian *bobo** (the word has no feminine form, but there are as many women *bobos* as men) is both easy to spot and hard to define.

1. *Bobos* are not really rich, but they earn a good living, often in so-called 'creative' jobs: literary journalist, designer, translator – not financial adviser or car dealer.
2. They often live in 'popular' neighbourhoods, i.e. ones with a mixed population, where Blacks and Arabs are well represented. But the neighbourhood is pleasant: no way would a *bobo* live near a motorway junction. As a result, the choice is rather limited: the banks of the Canal Saint-Martin, Belleville (the lower part, not Place des Fêtes), Barbès for some time now, Stalingrad, Aligre... Since *bobos* are numerous, their concentration in these places pushes up rents, which drives out the poor. Without meaning to, they end up among themselves. Though not living in groups – they are rather individualist – they go to the same cafés, the same shops. The more lucid are capable of making fun of themselves.
3. *Bobos* eat organic food, they frequent specialist fruit and vegetable shops selling local produce. They may be vegans, they may eat gluten-free bread, quinoa, and other supposedly healthy – and certainly expensive – foods. They are very careful about what they eat.
4. *Bobos* do not use a car in Paris. If they have one, it stays in the garage except for holidays. They ride bicycles, they walk, and, if they have to, they take public transport.

---

* A contraction of *bourgeois bohème* – Translator.

5. Politically, *bobos* are 'on the left', rather greenish, but never on the side of violence. They are feminist, anti-racist, concerned about the condition of animals; they sometimes go on demonstrations but they are not bold: they step aside when things start to heat up. They are the base of the electorate of the current mayor of Paris, Anne Hidalgo.

Jacobins

The Rue and Place Saint-Honoré should really be named after the Club des Jacobins. It was here that the famous club was established in 1789, in the library of the Jacobins convent, which was entered from Rue Saint-Honoré. These premises were destroyed after the Thermidor coup.

The fashion today is to oppose the Jacobins, supporters of Parisian dictatorship, in favour of the Girondins as apostles of decentralization. This is a historical untruth that is part of a vast operation aimed at discrediting the French Revolution. The Jacobins club had its headquarters in Paris, but its strength lay in its hundreds of branches throughout the country. The relationship between the Paris club and its affiliates was a two-way street. Abbé Grégoire recounts in his *Mémoires*:

> It was agreed that one of us would seek a suitable opportunity to raise this question during a session of the National Assembly. He was sure to be applauded by a very small number and booed by the majority; no matter, he asked and was granted referral to a committee where our opponents hoped to bury the question. The Jacobins took it up in their circular invitations and in their newspapers, it was discussed by four or five hundred affiliated societies, and three weeks later addresses poured in to the Assembly, demanding a decree that had initially been rejected in draft, but which it then accepted by a large majority, because the discussion had matured public opinion.

The Jacobins were a two-way system for spreading revolutionary ideas between Paris and the provinces.

And were the Girondins decentralizers? Most of them were elected officials from the provinces, they didn't know Paris, which frightened them, but that's not the same thing. Guy Debord recalls this in *Panegyric*:

> The infamous Isnard [deputy of the Var] presiding over the Convention in May 1793, had already had the impudence to announce prematurely: 'I say that if through these incessant insurrections the national representatives should happen to be attacked – I declare to you, in the name of all of France, Paris will be annihilated; you would soon search the banks of the Seine to determine whether this city ever existed."

It would be difficult to express hatred and fear any better.

The Girondins were high bourgeois, champions of laissez-faire, opposed to laws setting a maximum price for basic necessities. They had nothing but contempt for the people: 'What Babylon ever presented the spectacle of this Paris, stained with blood and debauchery, governed by magistrates who make a profession of spouting lies, peddling slander, advocating murder? What people has ever corrupted its morals and instincts to the point of contracting the need to see torments, and trembling with rage when they are delayed?' Madame Roland wrote this from prison, and she was one of the most endearing characters of her group. To support the Girondins, as our leaders do today, is to still fear the French Revolution after more than two centuries.

---

* Guy Debord, *Panegyric* (London: Verso, 1994), chapter IV.

Immeubles-Industriels,
Marcel Rajman

In his *Arcades Project*, Walter Benjamin asks, 'The Rue des Immeubles-Industriels, when does it date from?' The street was well designed to attract the attention of this attentive walker, but he did not have time enough to answer his question.

Stretching between the final few metres of Rue du Faubourg-Saint-Antoine and Boulevard Voltaire, very close to Place de la Nation, the street was first called Rue de l'Industrie-Saint-Antoine. Its architect, Émile Lemesnil (also responsible for the Bouffes-du-Nord) parcelled out the site and built this street in the early 1870s. Its two sides, which are absolutely identical, are each made up of seventeen buildings, likewise identical, for artisanal use. Each of these buildings has an industrial part – a ground floor with a mezzanine and two basements – and above this three levels of housing for its workers. The complex was designed as an extension to the neighbouring Faubourg Saint-Antoine, meaning that it was dedicated to the manufacture of wooden furniture. The energy required for the machines was supplied by a single source, a powerful steam engine from Cail, the great locomotive manufacturer of the time. The machine, located in the middle of the street, transmitted energy to the workshops through a system of articulated shafts located in the lower basement via an underground tunnel across the street. Each workshop could connect as needed to the shaft that passed through it. This system was not quite exceptional. Privat d'Anglemont explains in *Paris Anecdote* (1885):

It is one of those big cities in abbreviated form that you find in industrial districts and is called a *courtyard*. There are about fifteen of them in the Faubourg du Temple ... The owner, a large manufacturer, has built a steam engine for his factory there; but wanting to attract small manufacturers, he has had the shaft of his machine cross through all the ground floors, that is to say a length of one hundred and a few metres, and rents to each of his tenants, together with the dwelling, a belt to which they can affix a machine.

On either side of the street, each of the seventeen units has three identical bays. The ground floor and mezzanine are framed by a pair of cast-iron columns topped by a small Ionic capital. The mezzanine windows are bordered with bricks of a beautiful purplish red colour, combining subtly with the cast iron and glass. The present-day activities in the street are discreet: no shops, but architects, graphic designers and an art gallery; with just a few patches of colour that suggest a respect for this exceptional setting.

At building number 1 on the street, a plaque reads: 'Here lived Marcel Rajman, FTP-MOI,* one of the 23 of the *Affiche rouge*,† shot at Mont-Valérien on 21 February 1944 at the age of 21.' (There were twenty-two *résistants* shot that day, though only ten of them appear on the poster, including Rajman: 'Polish Jew, 13 attacks').

Between the two wars, Rue des Immeubles-Industriels became a centre of attraction for Jews from the East, and Yiddish was spoken there more than French. Marcel was eight years old when his family moved here – father Moszek, mother Chana and brother Simon. Under the occupation, he joined the Union of Jewish Youth, led by Henri Krasucki, then the resistance organisation FTP-MOI which included immigrants

---

* *'Main d'œuvre immigrée'* (Immigrant Labour) was a wing of the Communist-led armed resistance *'Francs-tireurs et partisans'* (Snipers and Partisans). – Translator.

† This 'red poster' featuring ten most wanted members of the FTP-MOI 'army of crime' was widely displayed on Paris walls in the spring of 1944.

from all over, Italians, Armenians, Hungarians and Poles, most of these Jews like Rajman. When he was just twenty years old, Marcel joined its Équipe spéciale, the spearhead of the armed struggle. In *Le Sang de l'étranger* (1989), Stéphane Courtois, Denis Peschanski and Adam Rayski recount two operations carried out by the team, out of several dozen. One was aimed at no less a figure than the *Kommandant* of the Paris region, General von Schaumberg. Cristina Boïco, head of the FTP intelligence service, had noticed that the general habitually rode his horse in the Bois de Boulogne before returning to his home on Avenue Raphaël, where his official car would arrive to take him to his offices at the Hôtel Meurice on Rue de Rivoli. On 28 July, the attack took place at the corner of Rue Nicolo and Avenue Paul-Doumer, led by four members of the Équipe spéciale, Kneler, Fontano, Kojitski and Rajman. At 9.30 a.m. the car arrived as planned and Kneler threw his grenade; there was a strong explosion and the team dispersed, thinking they had succeeded. However, it was not General von Schaumberg in the car but a member of his staff, and moreover the grenade had exploded behind the car and not inside it. The attack failed, but the team didn't give up. The same Cristina Boïco noted the address of an important dignitary whom a large Mercedes with a swastika pennant came to pick up each morning from his home on Rue Pétrarque behind the Trocadéro. Boris Holban, in charge of FTP-MOI military operations, reported:

> The scenario is prepared. [Rajman] is to watch for the man to leave, pass him on the street as he enters the car, shoot him and continue on his way without stopping. Alfonso is to follow him a few steps away and finish the job if necessary. Fontano will stand on the opposite pavement and see to defence. The dispersal routes are established. Everything has been calculated to the second.

The operation took place on 28 September 1943 under the authority of Missak Manouchian, who had replaced Holban. Alfonso fired first, the man inside the car was wounded and tried to get out through the opposite door but Rajman shot him three times. At the time, the team did not know the identity of their victim, but would soon learn that it was *Generalbevollmächtigter* Ritter, head of the STO (compulsory labour service for young Frenchmen sent to Germany) and a personal friend of Hitler.

From the summer of that year, however, Marcel Rajman had been spotted visiting his mother's house on Boulevard Soult. He was tailed by the BS2, the French special brigade, and arrested on 16 November on Rue Paul-Brousse, near Porte de Clichy, as part of a big haul which brought down sixty-eight militants (the BS2 summary report distinguished thirty-three 'Aryans' including nineteen foreigners, and thirty-four Jews including thirty foreigners). On 15 February 1944, twenty-four of these – the hard-core FTP-MOI fighters – were judged by a German court-martial. The prosecutor demanded death for twenty-three of the defendants. On 21 February, twenty-two men, including Marcel Rajman, were shot at Mont-Valérien. The only woman, Olga Bancic, was sent to Germany where she was beheaded with an axe in Stuttgart on her thirty-second birthday. The headline in *Paris-Soir* read: 'The Immigrant Workers' Movement was led by Jews who took their orders from Moscow', followed by the subhead: 'Manouchian, man of 150 murders.'

Domes

The oldest dome built in Paris (1608) is so small and well hidden that only a few people know it. It is on what was the chapel of the former convent of the Petits Augustins, which during the Revolution was the Museum of French Monuments and now serves as an exhibition hall for the École des Beaux-Arts on Quai Malaquais. To the right of the nave is the Chapelle des Louanges [Chapel of Praises], with a hexagonal footprint and covered with a dome, 'according to Félibien, the first built in this form to be seen in Paris'. It is very small and flat, with nothing to distinguish it from the outside.

Along the noble curve of Rue Saint-Antoine (mentally including Rue François-Miron which was the original part of this street) there are two remarkable domes to admire. The oldest is that of the church of Saint-Paul, the foundation stone of which was laid by Louis XIII in 1627 and which was completed in 1641. At that time, it was named after Saint-Louis; it was the church of the Jesuits and its architects were two members of that order, Fr. Derand and Fr. Martellange (who had very contrasting views regarding the plans of the church and its façade).

From the street, you can hardly see the dome, which is hidden by a tall three-storey façade, probably inspired by the neighbouring church of Saint-Gervais. This is an initial clumsiness – and a notable difference from the Gesù in Rome, model of all Jesuit churches, where the façade does not hide the dome. To see the dome of Saint-Paul, you have to go through the small Rue du Prévôt and Rue Charlemagne to reach the Saint-Paul gardens. It is hexagonal and topped by a lantern. But the six-panel drum is too high in relation to the size of the dome: you sense here a certain archaism, the clumsiness of architects with no experience in this field, but it is a clumsiness full of charm, like the too long neck of a young girl – a comparison which would probably not have pleased Fathers Derand and Martellange.

The other dome on Rue Saint-Antoine is that of the church of the Visitation, near the Bastille. It is scarcely more recent (begun in 1632), but its architect was a genius, François Mansart. The footprint of this church is a circle within a square. The façade, accessed by a small flight of steps, is pierced by a door inscribed in a large arch and surmounted by a triangular pediment in the antique style (on the sides of the pediment, the nineteenth century added two statues that are more Ovid than holy writ). The dome, which emerges from a four-sided roof, rests on a drum supported by eight buttresses. It is surmounted by a lantern topped by a spherical cap with an arrow. Its proportions are in perfect harmony with the rest of the building. The eye is led from the entrance steps to the lantern without a break, the whole being at once massive and slender, compact and elegant: the very image of perfection. It is the only Mansart building in Paris that has not been demolished or altered. Since 1803, it has been a Protestant church.

I know of only one other dome that is equally successful: the church of the Salpêtrière hospital. This rises in the middle of the two large wings designed by Le Vau. When Le Vau died, the work was entrusted to Libéral Bruant, principal architect of the Invalides. The church is in the shape of a Greek cross, a large octagonal rotunda with four naves. Chapels in the corners of the naves allowed for a separation of social strata and genders, but all with a view of the choir. The dome, built on a wooden frame, stands above the large arcades of the rotunda; it is octagonal, covered with slate like the roof. Its drum is pierced by eight large windows and is surmounted by a lantern. Here, it is not slenderness that has been sought, but solidity and calm, in keeping with the purpose of the place.

There are many other domes in Paris, that of the Invalides, whose gold stands out in the synoptic view of Paris

from Montmartre, that of Saint-Joseph-des-Carmes on Rue
de Vaugirard, that of the chapel of the Sorbonne where Richelieu's tomb is located, that of Notre-Dame-de-l'Assomption
on Rue Saint-Honoré, so heavy and clumsy that Parisians
called it 'the woozy dome', and the one in Val-de-Grâce, which
Bernini once called 'a very small skullcap for such a big head'
(he liked nothing in Paris except the Innocents fountain with
its sculptures by Jean Goujon). I'm sure to have forgotten
some, but will end with the one that is probably most recent:
that of the Panthéon, which dates from the 1770s and is, I
believe, the only major dome built in Paris in the eighteenth
century. At the time, its very large dimensions raised doubts
about its solidity. (In the heated controversies on this subject,
it is perhaps necessary to bring in the fact that Soufflot was
from Lyon and the Parisian architects probably took a dim
view of this great construction site.) The dome here rests on a
double drum: the lower part is a broad colonnade that blends
in perfectly with the rest of the building, while the upper part,
inscribed in the first but with a much smaller radius, supports
the dome – which is, as a result, far too small in relation to the
mass of the building. Was Soufflot afraid that a dome of the
right proportions would be too heavy? Or did he not realize
the mistake until it was too late? We'll never know.

Before the computer, it was probably difficult to imagine
what a dome would look like once it was finished. So many
elements come into play – the volume in relation to the rest
of the building, the height of the drum and its diameter, the
curvature of the surface – that it took the eye of a Mansart to
bring them together in harmonious synthesis.

Squares*

Most Parisian *squares* date from the nineteenth century, and many were designed by Adolphe Alphand, the great landscape architect who strove to make Haussmann's mineral universe breathable. I will only talk about the ones that I find most beautiful.

In the Marais, Rues Saint-Gilles and Payenne form a right angle, and on each side of this angle a *square* opens up. The more charming of the two is Square Georges Cain (named after a former curator of the Carnavalet museum) which abuts Rue Payenne. The grounds were part of the gardens of the Hôtel Saint-Fargeau, whose rear façade borders the back of the *square* behind a row of lime trees (the Saint-Fargeau family were *noblesse de robe*, one of them had been 'provost of merchants', the equivalent of a mayor, while the last and most famous was stabbed by a bodyguard of Louis XVI while dining alone at the Février restaurant in the Palais-Royal). To the left (north) is the magnificent orangery of this *hôtel* – the only one in Paris – designed, like the *hôtel* itself, by Pierre Bullet, architect of Porte Saint-Martin and the church of Saint-Thomas-d'Aquin. Opposite, on the south wall, there are various vestigial marbles from Parisian history, notably the pediment of the central pavilion of the Tuileries palace, burnt down in 1871. In the centre of the garden, a Maillol statue stands in a flowerbed, a naked woman holding a towel behind her back. This calm and welcoming *square* is an ideal halt in the hustle and bustle of the Marais.

---

* The English word 'square' covers both a *square* and a *place*. A *square* in the French sense, however, is traffic-free and fenced, with elements of a public garden. – Translator.

Stretching between Boulevard de Sébastopol and Rue Saint-Martin, opposite the main entrance to the Conservatoire des Arts et Métiers, Square Émile-Chautemps (formerly Square des Arts et Métiers) is an oasis of greenery in a neighbourhood that hardly has any. Two water features along its axis are each decorated with bronze groups associating two figures: on the left (looking towards Arts et Métiers) Agriculture and Industry, on the right Mercury and Music. A stream of water gushes out between the figures and the whole is surrounded by a lawn and encircled by a fence with a superb design. You are free to find it either kitsch or charming. In the centre of the *square*, a granite column bears on each side of its base the name of a French victory during the Crimean War (Sébastopol, Alma, Inkerman and Tchernaïa – which means 'black' in Russian, the battle taking place on the 'black river'). This *square* is a pleasant junction between two neighbourhoods, on one side the Sentier (across Boulevard de Sébastopol you are on Rue du Caire) and on the other the small neighbourhood of Arts et Métiers, whose streets bear the names of sometimes forgotten inventors: Papin, Vaucanson, Conté (creator of the pencil), Montgolfier, Volta … all names from the happy time when science was a friend who did not harm anyone.

With the magnificent scenography of the church of Saint-Vincent-de-Paul and the big concrete X's of the bridge over the railway tracks from the Gare de l'Est, Square Montholon is one of those accidents that break the monotony of the long Rue Lafayette. (Lafayette, whom the French adore. They forget – or never knew – that, in August 1792, he crossed over to the enemy with all his staff, high treason if ever there was such.) The square is equipped with benches around the trunks of the immense plane trees, which provide shade and coolness even in the middle of summer. More or less in the centre is a sculpted group remarkable both for its quality (rare among the countless statues in *squares*) and its theme: 'To the women workers of Paris' – not factory workers, in this case, but those of the fashion trade. The fencing around the *square* is also remarkable: low, cast iron, with heart-shaped motifs that the vegetation blends into. On the opposite side of Rue Lafayette, Rue Belfond crosses over Rue Pierre-Sémard on an iron bridge from which there is a beautiful view over the *square*.

My favourite, however, is Square Louvois, opposite the entrance to the Bibliothèque Nationale. Louvois had his *hôtel* nearby, and we find here three great ministers of the Ancien Régime: Richelieu, Louvois and Colbert, whose *hôtel* was located on a street along the north side of the Bibliothèque. (Parenthesis: there is talk of removing Colbert's bust in front of the National Assembly on the grounds that he was the author of the Code Noir. That would be too easy. Braver to take on the leaders of the mining, oil and other companies that perpetuate a slavery as deadly as that of the Code Noir.) From 1794 to 1820, the site of Square Louvois was occupied by the Opéra – hence the names of the surrounding streets, Lulli, Rameau, Méhul, Cherubini. It was destroyed in 1820 after Louvel, a Bonapartist worker, fatally stabbed the Duc de Berry, younger son of the Comte d'Artois (later Charles X) and heir presumptive to the throne.

In the centre of Square Louvois stands a graceful fountain depicting the four great rivers of France. It is the work of Visconti, best known for having designed Napoleon's tomb at the Invalides – and for a small street bearing his name, between Rue de Seine and Rue Bonaparte, where Balzac had his printing works.

Unlike their London counterparts, Parisian *squares* are closed at night. Could it be for fear of their serving to 'hide secret lecheries', as Baudelaire puts it? More likely for fear of their becoming refuges for the homeless, who would roll out their bundles to sleep in peace. Or worse, of their being squatted by 'migrants', Afghans or others, who might set up camp there. The closing of *squares* is a weapon in the war against the poor, an endless war in which Paris is an ever-changing battlefield.

Two Germans

Heinrich Heine and Walter Benjamin – two German Jews whose French trajectories, a hundred years apart, are not without common points.

In 1831, Heine's situation in Germany was not too good. His *Travel Pictures*, a virulent critique of the alliance of Prussian throne and altar, was condemned and seized by the police. His hopes of obtaining a municipal position in Hamburg evaporated. Without resources, and his writings censored, he decided to emigrate to France, where the revolution had just triumphed. He was thirty-four years old.

In 1933, Walter Benjamin had been living in Ibiza for a few months. In Nazi Germany, his brother had been arrested, Adorno expelled from Frankfurt University, his friends – Bertolt Brecht, Ernst Bloch – had emigrated. Benjamin abandoned the possibility of returning to his homeland and left for Paris, already familiar from two previous visits (he had translated there the beginning of Proust's magnum opus). He was forty-one years old.

Heine, when he arrived in Paris in May 1831, settled first on the Left Bank and then in the fashionable district near Notre-Dame-de-Lorette (see Patricia Baudoin's 2008 introduction to Heine's *Lutèce*). He frequented the people who mattered in the intellectual and artistic life of Paris: Balzac and George Sand, Liszt and Chopin, Thiers and Quinet. To earn a living, he sent articles to the *Augsburger Allgemeine Zeitung*, one of the highest circulation German daily newspapers. He was soon disappointed by the development of the new regime's promised 'middle way': 'Louis-Philippe has forgotten that his government was born from the principle of popular sovereignty; with distressing blindness he seeks to sustain himself by quasi-legitimacy, by alliances with absolute princes and by continuing the period of the Restoration (28 December 1831)'. Heine later related in his own way the cholera epidemic of 1832:

> By the great misery that reigns here, by the terrible filth that can be found not only among the poorest classes, above all by the irritability of the people and their boundless flippancy, by the total lack of preventive measures, cholera was able to spread with greater swiftness and horror than anywhere else. Its arrival was officially announced on 29 March, and as this was the mid-Lent holiday, with sunshine and charming weather, Parisians celebrated all the more merrily on the boulevards; you could even see masks which, parodying the sickly colour and ravaged face, mocked the fear of cholera and the disease itself (19 April 1832).

On the republican uprising of June 1832: 'It was the best blood which ran in Rue Saint-Martin, and I do not believe that there was better fighting at Thermopylae than at the mouth of the alleys of Saint-Merri and Aubry-le-Boucher, where at the last a handful of some sixty Republicans fought against sixty thousand troops of the line and National Guards, and twice beat them back (15 June 1832)'. He reported on the Salon of 1833: 'Like Louis-Philippe in politics, M. Ingres was this year the king in art; as the former reigns at the Tuileries, he reigned at the Louvre. The character of M. Ingres is also a middle way; M. Ingres is indeed a middle way between Miéris and Michelangelo.'

Heine's articles were systematically censored in Germany, so he brought them together, restored to their original virulence, in a volume entitled *Französische Zustände* (*French Conditions*). At the same time, he published a study on German literature and philosophy, *Religion and Philosophy in Germany*, in which he redressed in particular the image of Hegelianism, seen in France through Victor Cousin's spectacles. The book was a failure and closed the doors of Paris publishers for him, while his writings were still banned in Germany. So as not to die of hunger, he was forced to resume his collaboration with the *Augsburger Allgemeine Zeitung*. His subjects ranged from Meyerbeer to Spontini, Guizot to Thiers, the Eastern question, the fortifications being built around Paris and the erection of the Luxor obelisk. Heine brought together these pieces under the title *Lutetia*, published in Germany in 1854. In the preface he explains the reasons for this publication: 'These letters having appeared anonymously in the *Allgemeine Zeitung*, and not without having undergone notable deletions and changes, I was bound to fear they would be published after my death in this faulty form.' If he spoke of dying, this was because he was already in an advanced stage of the illness that would carry him off in 1856, after eight years on his Parisian 'divan-tomb'.

When Benjamin arrived in Paris, he stayed first of all at a small hotel (the Palace) on the corner of Rue du Four and Boulevard Saint-Germain. He moved several times, looking for cheaper and more suitable accommodation, but always on the Left Bank. His financial situation was disastrous: 'I've been lying there for days – just so as to need nothing and see no one – and I work as best I can. Think about what you can get for me. I need 1,000 francs for the most urgent matters and to get through March', he wrote in February 1934 to his friend Gretel Karplus, wife of Theodor Adorno. He was finally saved when the Institut für Sozialforschung, which had emigrated from Frankfurt to Geneva – and then to Amsterdam before settling finally in New York – managed through Max Horkheimer to pay him a monthly retainer of 1,500 francs. This was to enable him to pursue his *Arcades Project*. Adorno wrote to him on 6 November 1934: 'I truly consider this work a piece of *prima philosophia* entrusted to us, and my dearest wish is to see you now, after a long and painful stalemate, master the execution that this immense object requires.'

Benjamin hardly saw anyone, but he had found the place that would be his nest for a number of years, 'one of the most curious libraries on earth, where you work as in an opera set ... Since I started going out again, I actually spend all day there in the reading room, and I've pretty much settled into the baffling rules' (to Adorno, 9 March 1934). Benjamin plunged ahead with the *Arcades*, but it soon became clear that Adorno, his main intermediary with the Institute, did not properly understand this work. After receiving, in 1935, an initial presentation, a kind of summary of the work to come, he sent Benjamin long letters, friendly and respectful but clearly critical:

> your preoccupation now must be to renounce interpretation; the material, once presented, speaks for itself; however you cannot dispense with the Institute, and the approach must therefore be adapted to it ... I would like to urge you to write the Arcades in accordance with their own origins. My deepest conviction is that the work will only gain from this, even and especially in Marxist terms (20 May 1935).

And on receipt of a new section:

> Can you understand that reading this essay, its chapter entitled 'The Flâneur' and even the other one, 'Modernity', produced in me a certain disappointment? The main reason for this is that, in the parts I have read, the work offers less a model than a prelude to the Arcades. The themes are brought together but not developed. In your letter to Max [Horkheimer], you say that this was your explicit intention, and I do not underestimate the ascetic discipline you have imposed on yourself to avoid everywhere giving decisive theoretical responses to questions, even to make the questions themselves perceptible only to the initiated (10 November 1938).

The misunderstanding increased as time went by. From 1937 onwards, Benjamin changed his project: the Baudelaire chapter planned for the *Arcades* book grew to such a scope that it was gradually transformed into an autonomous book that 'phagocytized' everything else (see Giorgio Agamben's introduction to this book, reconstructed from fragments).* Benjamin took this turn without clearly explaining it to the Institute, on which he depended financially and which he was forced to handle carefully even at the price of clarity.

When war broke out, Benjamin was interned on 5 September 1939 as a German refugee, first in the Colombes stadium where he remained for ten days, then in the Vernuche camp near Nevers. His friends (in particular Adrienne Monnier) intervened with Henri Hoppenot, head of the Europe desk at the foreign ministry, who had him released on 16 November. Benjamin returned to Paris. On 23 May 1940, it was decided that all German refugees would now be interned, but, once again, Hoppenot intervened effectively on his behalf. On 11 January 1941, Benjamin wrote to his friend Gershom Scholem: 'Every line we can publish today is – so uncertain the future to which we dispatch them – a victory snatched from the powers of darkness'.† And Benjamin would find the energy to write his *Theses on the Concept of History* (probably in May 1940), conceived as a 'theoretical framework for the second essay on Baudelaire' and which lovers of Benjamin know almost by heart.

On 13 May 1940, the day before German troops entered Paris, Benjamin took the train to Lourdes. From there he continued to Marseille and then Port-Vendres, with the intention of crossing into Spain. With two other German refugees, he walked to Portbou, a small village in the north of Catalonia, just over the border. But on learning that the Spanish government had ordered fugitives to be deported to France, he killed himself on 26 September by taking a large dose of the morphine he had with him to relieve the pain in his back.

* Giorgio Agamben, *On Benjamin's Baudelaire* (University Press Scholarship Online, 2016).

† *The Correspondence of Walter Benjamin* (Chicago: University of Chicago Press, 1994).

Street Sounds

This morning, a travelling musician came up my street – a very talented trumpeter who played with a single hand, the other pulling a cart that produced his orchestral accompaniment. In my youth, you often saw and heard street musicians, as well as men (always men) who cried their trade from the pavements: grinders, builders, glaziers. In 'The Glass-Vendor', Baudelaire recounts that, one day, he heard a glass-vendor 'whose shrill and discordant cry mounted up to me through the heavy, dull Parisian atmosphere'. Baudelaire had him carry his heavy burden up to the sixth floor, and when he arrived said to him: 'What? Have you no coloured glasses? Glasses of rose and crimson and blue, magical glasses, glasses of Paradise? You are insolent. You dare to walk in mean streets when you have no glasses that would make one see beauty in life?' And he hustled him to the staircase. Then, from the balcony, he threw a flowerpot which broke 'his poor walking fortune. It made a noise like a palace of crystal shattered by lightning.'

Proust was not a great walker in Paris, but had an incomparable ear for the sounds of the city. From his bed he could tell the weather from the sound of the tram on the boulevard. And in *The Captive*:

Here again it was of the barely lyrical declamation of Moussorgsky that the vendor reminded me, but not of it alone. For after having almost 'spoken': '*Les escargots, ils sont frais, ils sont beaux,*' it was with the vague melancholy of Maeterlinck, transposed into music by Debussy, that the snail vendor, in one of those pathetic finales in which the composer of *Pelléas* shows his kinship with Rameau: 'If vanquished I must be, is it for thee to be my vanquisher?' added with a singsong melancholy: '*On les vend six sous la douzaine...*'

Index

INDEX